UNIVERSITY OF NORTH CAROLINA AT CHAPEL HILL
DEPARTMENT OF ROMANCE LANGUAGES

NORTH CAROLINA STUDIES
IN THE ROMANCE LANGUAGES AND LITERATURES

Founder: URBAN TIGNER HOLMES

Editors: MARÍA A. SALGADO
CAROL L. SHERMAN

Distributed by:

UNIVERSITY OF NORTH CAROLINA PRESS

CHAPEL HILL
North Carolina 27515-2288
U.S.A.

NORTH CAROLINA STUDIES IN THE
ROMANCE LANGUAGES AND LITERATURES
Number 254

THE AESTHETICS OF ARTIFICE:
VILLIERS'S *L'EVE FUTURE*

THE AESTHETICS OF ARTIFICE: VILLIERS'S *L'EVE FUTURE*

BY
MARIE LATHERS

CHAPEL HILL

NORTH CAROLINA STUDIES IN THE ROMANCE
LANGUAGES AND LITERATURES
U.N.C. DEPARTMENT OF ROMANCE LANGUAGES

1996

Library of Congress Cataloging-in-Publication Data

Lathers, Marie
    The aesthetics of artifice: Villiers's L'Eve future / by Marie Lathers.
    p. – cm. – (North Carolina Studies in the Romance Languages & Literatures; no. 254).
    Includes bibliographical references.
    ISBN 0-8078-9258-0 (alk. paper).
    1. Villiers de L'Isle-Adam, Auguste, comte de, 1838-1889. Eve future. I. Title. II. Series.

PQ2476.V4E9235   1996   96-14848
843'.8 – dc20   CIP

Cover: Jean-Léon Gérôme, *The Artist and His Model*. From the Haggin Collection. The Haggin Museum, Stockton, California. By permission.

Cover design: Shelley Gruendler

© 1996. Department of Romance Languages. The University of North Carolina at Chapel Hill.

ISBN 0-8078-9254-8

IMPRESO EN ESPAÑA

PRINTED IN SPAIN

DEPÓSITO LEGAL: V. 353 - 1997

ARTES GRÁFICAS SOLER, S. A. - LA OLIVERETA, 28 - 46018 VALENCIA

CONTENTS

	Page
FOREWORD: *Tekhné*: State of the Art and *L'Eve future* by John Anzalone	9
PREFACE	13
ACKNOWLEDGMENTS	17
INTRODUCTION	19
CHAPTER 1: Representational Texts	27
[A] Bride of Frankenstein	29
[B] Chefs-d'oeuvre	36
CHAPTER 2: Photosculpture	46
CHAPTER 3: Sculpture	56
[A] Statues	58
[B] Grounding Sculpture	65
[C] The Hypnotic Feminine	73
CHAPTER 4: Photography	85
[A] Photogenic Women	87
[B] Maternal Photographs	93
[C] Moving Pictures	102
CHAPTER 5: Early Images of Psychoanalysis	111
[A] Technologies of the Feminine	112
[B] Aura Hysterica	118
[C] Saxa Loquuntur!	124
CONCLUSION	137
WORKS CITED	143

FOREWORD

TEKHNÉ: STATE OF THE ART AND *L'EVE FUTURE*

Defiantly unconventional, despite his deep-seated traditionalism, Auguste de Villiers de l'Isle-Adam produced a body of writing so uncomfortable for canonically determined hierarchies that for a time it seemed in danger of disappearing altogether. Absent for the most part from the scholarly manuals, briefly dispensed with in the literary histories, Villiers survived thanks to a handful of lucid critics, and via something akin to a literary underground: his important works, passed along by previous initiates in whatever out-of-print editions could be had, continued to find new enthusiastic readers; most were without a care for the standard verdict that here was a marginal writer, an author of flawed, minor works.

As prevailing definitions have been called into question, Villiers has at last found a place on university reading lists and yet another audience. It's an audience that has, in a sense, caught up with him. Emergent critical and theoretical practices that have challenged canonicity by their focus on oppositional discourse or marginality have prepared new readers to hear in Villiers's writings a prophetic voice that brings the *fin de siècle révolté* far closer to us. The focus has been sharpened and brought to bear on some of the deeper, more troubling aspects of his works. It is in this context that one of them has achieved a special prominence: *L'Eve future*, the story of the creation by a scientist, a lover, and "state of the art" technology of an android woman in the name of impenitent idealism. This disturbing, prescient and utterly original work moves quickly and deeply into the type of controlled delirium that the surrealists hailed as a font of truth. Never before in his career had Villiers sustained both abstract complexity and visionary lyricism so thoroughly. *L'Eve future* confronts with breathtaking focus central taboos and ambivalences of the decadent period that we still find pressing today. Questions about the power and limits of machines and science over the human capacity to think and experience the real, questions of sexuality, of desire, and of gender are raised with the express purpose of shattering comfortable categories, and no wonder: a real woman resembling a work of art but deemed spiritually deficient by her lover is replaced by an artificial device resembling a woman – but spiritually more satisfying – by an inventor.

This extended foray into the uncanny theorizes a nineteenth-century *tekhné*, an intimate identification of art and technology to achieve the new woman. It is this nexus that Marie Lathers has untangled from the critically central perspective of gender in *The Aesthetics of Artifice*. Relatively little of the recently abundant critical literature on *L'Eve future* treats in an explicit theoretical context what she calls its "sexual politics." Yet, as she demonstrates, the dominant bourgeois ideologies – in and of themselves Villiers's favorite satirical targets – of the nineteenth century in France, when subsumed by the technological marvels so often foregrounded in his writing, result in *L'Eve future* in a programmatic remapping of the feminine.

No serious reader of *L'Eve future* can remain indifferent to the extensive, astonishing dissection of the robot Hadaly in book 5, with its many attendant and subversive suggestions on how to improve on the original female body when constructing its replica. The female body is, inescapably, the privileged locus of the exploration carried out in *L'Eve future* and Marie Lathers impresses upon us the centrality of that fact. In carefully ordered chapters that take us incrementally from image and representation to simulation and replication, she identifies the experimenter's tools as photosculpture, three-dimensional sculptural modelling, photography, and cinema; and she finds the language required for the user's manual for the resulting artificial dream doll – or is it a "boy-toy"? – in the nascent medical discourses and demonstrations of hysteria and psychoanalysis.

She has thus given us a full-length study of *L'Eve future* (only the second ever, incidentally) that does not simply replace the novel in the most significant historical contexts of nineteenth century artistic and technological developments, but that uses those developments with authentic cross-disciplinary insight to resituate and better decipher its ideological discourse on the feminine. Drawing on the novel's central metaphor of the statue of the *Venus de Milo* as the representation of the perfect woman, she explores, for example, the powerful implications inherent in the similarities between the model's pose in the sculptor's atelier and the hysteric's positioning in the clinical demonstrations of J.-M. Charcot. Or again, sculptural representation is examined in its relationship to hypnosis and paralysis in a pertinent rereading of Freud.

Critics have long understood the fascination with science and technology as a fundamental aspect of Villiers's particular genius. *The Aesthetics of Artifice* concentrates on how in *L'Eve future*, via Edison and Ewald, science and art share ways of imaging woman that bind her, petrify her, and render her inert for their ministrations. Modernity's ways of "imaging" woman call upon the new technologies of mechanical reproduction of originals that promote the artificial feminine at the expense of real woman: as Marie Lathers notes, "modern images do not merely represent, they literally cancel out." At a critical moment in the novel, when Lord Ewald reaches the end of a lengthy, imagined monologue to be recited by the soul-sister his mistress Alicia Clary can never become, this ventriloquist has his phantom woman cry out in melancholy consolation, "L'art seul efface et délivre" – "Art alone erases and delivers." Spoken by this hypothetical woman, these verbs have no objects; when they have as subject the discourse of the state of the art technologies Marie Lathers has so revealingly analyzed in *The Aesthetics of Artifice*, their object is woman.

JOHN ANZALONE
Skidmore College

PREFACE

At the end of his 1933 lecture entitled *Femininity*, Sigmund Freud advises, "If you want to know more about femininity, enquire from your own experiences of life, or turn to the poets, or wait until science can give you deeper and more coherent information" (22: 135). I have followed two of these suggestions by turning to a symbolist writer, and in particular to his major prose work, *L'Eve future*. The study of this text has also entailed an inquiry into science, in the form of technology. One need not wait, however, for science to provide further insight into femininity, for the science of the past is rich in its various constructions of woman. And it is precisely these past technologies that provide in large part the foundations of theories of the feminine such as Freud's own.

My initial design in writing on *L'Eve future* was twofold: first, I wanted to valorize a text that deserves a more prominent place in class syllabi and the pages of literary criticism; second, I wished to discover the ideological underpinnings, aesthetic and scientific, of nineteenth-century France's fictional fabrication of woman. This project seemed on the one hand entirely feasible – after all, *L'Eve future*, with its detailed narration of a very literal construction of woman, lends itself to such an endeavor. On the other hand, the task appeared overwhelming precisely because of the vastness of Villiers's own undertaking, which opposes the artificial ideal to several unacceptable versions of woman (including the bourgeois beauty, the *femme fatale*, and the somnambulist hysteric), thus creating not one or two but several versions of the feminine. As I argue in the pages that follow, each of these nineteenth-century feminine types must be examined in detail, for each is in a very real sense an integral part of Villiers's deconstruction of an Eve who is all too human and his subsequent construction of a brave new Eve.

It occurred to me early on that Hadaly, Villiers's android, was to be above all an aesthetic masterpiece, a Galatea modeled after the *Venus de Milo*. But in addition the android was to represent modernity through her status as a technical object and image (she is a bibelot and a photograph). The android thus reconciles the contradictions of Baudelaire's ideal work of art: she is a classical statue *and* a product of the modern eye. The female of the future thus represents the introduction of technology into the history of art, rewriting art history as an aesthetics of artifice. It follows that the influence of technology on the image, and especially on images of woman, is of major concern in this study. That technology in its monstrous forms has been gendered as feminine at the same time that it restricts female reproductive capacities raises significant questions concerning the relationship among representation, reproduction, and maternity. If this study adds pertinently to current discussion of these issues it will have fulfilled its task.

The title *The Aesthetics of Artifice* refers to three concepts that promote the ideology behind the construction of a new Eve: aesthetics, artifice, and the artificial. Edison is an aesthetician or philosopher of aesthetics, the "science" of art or beauty; Ewald is the aesthete who idolizes beauty; Hadaly is the aesthetic product of their philosophizing and inventing, a being who represents the beautiful and sublime as opposed to the pleasing or utilitarian. Villiers's aesthetics is an aesthetics of the feminine, which in its modern form is an artifice, an invention or product of trickery that collapses the distinction between the sincere and insincere, the factual and the factitious. The idea of artifice leads, in turn, to the artificial, that which is opposed to nature and fabricated through human effort: the simulated, the synthetic, the feigned, the conventionalized, the imitation, the sham. In this production of the artificial, Edison assumes the role of artificer, the skilled imitator of nature.

Chapter 1 summarizes the invention of woman fictionalized in numerous nineteenth-century texts, since a conception of woman as the fragmented specimen of artistic and scientific revision was well-established in France and Europe before the publication of *L'Eve future*. These artificial women – from the destroyed female mate of Frankenstein's monster and the animated Galateas of Balzac, to Gautier's rejuvenated mummies – are Hadaly's maternal ancestors. In addition, a post-*L'Eve future* novel, Jules Verne's *Le Château des*

Carpathes is an example of the influence Villiers exerted on his contemporaries, an influence that continues into the twentieth century.

Chapter 2 is a brief detailed analysis of the fundamental process applied in the cloning of Hadaly from her human model. Photosculpture, an actual technique employed in the nineteenth century for the reproduction of small statues, synthesizes the idealizing potentials of sculpture and photography. Lauded even by idealists such as Théophile Gautier, photosculpture represents in miniature, literally and figuratively, Villiers's entire project.

The status of sculpture as an instrument for the three-dimensional fabrication of the feminine is investigated in chapter 3. As a resurrected and restored modern version of the *Venus de Milo*, Hadaly represents, paradoxically, a unique and ideal example of a mass-produced artwork. Through readings of Quatremère de Quincy and Charles Baudelaire, a fantasized association is exposed among sculpture, death, and the feminine reinforced by Villiers's Hadaly. This chapter also proposes stratagems for a future theory of sculpture as text, a process long in place with respect to painting. The roles of hypnosis and paralysis in the novel, symptoms of hysteria investigated in the nineteenth century by J.-M. Charcot and Sigmund Freud, are then examined, and the relationship of these phenomena to sculptural representation is discussed.

Photography, the technical art of the nineteenth century, is queried in chapter 4 as a means of mechanical reproduction *par excellence*. Here I append Benjamin's fundamental essay by suggesting that photography does not banish aura from modernity, but rather establishes an "artificial aura" of family, genealogy, memory and history – a phenomenon that becomes apparent in a reading of Roland Barthes's *Camera Lucida*. Photography is, furthermore, a technique that constructs the ideal feminine from multiple and fragmented images of various women in need of retouching. Finally, the startling cinematic passage found in *L'Eve future* in which Edison (re)presents feminine artifice through successive photography is read in the context of current studies of the cinematic depiction of the female body and voice.

In chapter 5, these discussions of sculpture and photography are drawn together and the arts are exposed as privileged iconographic technologies contributing to what Michel Foucault has called the "hysterization" of woman. J.-M. Charcot's photographic studio, where the female hysterics of the Salpêtrière Hospital were systematically captured by the camera lens, has been interpreted recently as a "theater" in which hysteria was dramatized. I draw on this work and read *L'Eve future* as a literary example of the production of *aura hysterica*. Finally, returning to hypnosis, the sculptural iconography analyzed in two of Freud's texts is presented as a "return of the repressed" of his early advocacy of the cure by hypnosis.

This study's epilogue suggests that Edison's project is embedded in our current notions of the relationship between gender and technology, as *Blade Runner*, a recent film, is shown to contain eery echoes of *L'Eve future*.

ACKNOWLEDGMENTS

This book began as a Ph.D. dissertation completed at Brown University. I would like to thank Henry Majewski and Mary Ann Doane for their invaluable readings of it and for their kind support. I am especially grateful to Naomi Schor who directed the dissertation and has continued to offer support and guidance. My gratitude also goes to John Anzalone for his generous help with this and other Villiers projects since that time.

A Kenyon Fellowship from Brown University allowed me to finish the dissertation, and a summer stipend from the College of Sciences and Humanities at Iowa State University helped me accomplish its revision. Publication funding was generously offered by the College of Liberal Arts and Sciences, the Department of Foreign Languages and Literatures and the Women's Studies Program of Iowa State University. I would also like to thank Véronique Leroux-Hugon of the Bibliothèque Charcot in Paris for her assistance. The Haggin Museum kindly granted permission to reproduce the image on the cover.

María Salgado, Carol Sherman, Rick Fleming and Claire Magaha at the University of North Carolina were very supportive during the publication process, and I thank them.

Finally, I thank *The Romanic Review*, the *Australian Journal of French Studies* and the *Yearbook of Interdisciplinary Studies in the Fine Arts* for permission to reprint material here.

INTRODUCTION

In 1906, Léon Bloy characterized the essence of Villiers de l'Isle-Adam's creative undertaking in this way

> The central preoccupation, the umbilicus of the remarkable poet who was the author of *L'Eve future*, and what must be totally intolerable to imbeciles, was his really unheard of need for a *restitution* of Woman . . . he endeavored resolutely to create her, as a God would have, with mud and saliva. (10-11, trans. mine)

L'Eve future, published in 1886 by Villiers, the symbolist poet, playwright, and short story writer, is indeed the story of a very literal restitution of woman. From an imperfect model – a Lilith named Alicia – Thomas Edison designs and constructs an ideal Eve with the help of a sleepwalker named Sowana. The android will not only be the perfect mate for Edison's friend, Lord Ewald, but will serve as prototype for a new race of faultless women. Villiers's humorous and at times highly sarcastic text is at once an idealist's version of the creation of a new Eve and a biting criticism of his positivist society, a society on the road to believing that modern inventions can cure all ills. The dedication "Aux rêveurs, aux railleurs" ("To dreamers, to jeerers") sums up Villiers's standpoint: his witty jeering is also an admonition to dream.

One evening in 1883, Lord Celian Ewald, English aristocrat and dandy, arrives at the Menlo Park, New Jersey home of his friend Thomas Alva Edison to say farewell. Firmly convinced that Alica Clary, the only woman he can love, is incapable of attaining the spirituality he requires in a companion, Ewald is determined to take his own life. The American positivist and first-rate engineer Edison stalls Ewald with the following proposal: he will separate Miss Alicia's perfect body from her tainted soul and produce the android Hadaly, an Eve of the future who will fulfill Ewald's quest for the ideal and serve as prototype for a new artificial race of women. Edison and Ewald's lengthy discussion of this monstrous scheme forms the body of *L'Eve future* and introduces the reader to Villiers's views concerning everything from theater to music and medicine to mesmerism. As Hadaly slowly materializes, so, interestingly enough, does Alicia: the real woman arrives in Menlo Park to serve as model for Hadaly, and this presence eventually leads to Ewald's confusion of the two in the climactic garden scene of book 6.

Seemingly endless technical details matched with far-fetched supernatural pronouncements, all delivered in a tone alternating between the poetic ("dreamers") and downright hilarious ("jeerers"), are provided as Edison and his sleepwalking assistant, Sowana, piece together the metallic but nonetheless feminine Hadaly. After he initially confuses the two and crosses momentarily into a state of madness, Ewald chooses the artificial Hadaly as mate and prepares their departure, leaving Edison more than a little astonished at the all-too-real reflection of the feminine that he has created. A disaster at sea silences the ideal, however, as Hadaly sinks to the bottom of the ocean in the coffin that serves as her traveling case. Ewald, inconsolable, sends Edison a final telegram. His assistant Sowana already deceased – or transported to another realm – Edison sits alone and silent as the novel ends.

The transformation of Alicia into the ideal Hadaly involves an aesthetic and technological revision or restitution of the feminine. First, Hadaly incarnates the *Venus de Milo*, the nineteenth century's archetype of classical female beauty that is insufficiently reproduced in the form of Alicia. Only Hadaly, the copy of a copy, attains the spiritual transcendence expected of an animated chef-d'oeuvre. Second, Hadaly is a product of nineteenth-century technologies of transformation: she is an electromagnetic being who profits from many contemporary inventions, including the phonograph and photograph. Thus Villiers, the vehement anti-positivist, turns to science for a solution to a pressing problem – modern femininity. Since Hadaly, the Eve of the future, is both an *objet d'art* and an *objet technique*, *L'Eve future*'s construction of woman entails a thoroughly modern rewriting of art to accommodate a new technological discourse. The aesthetics of Villiers's construction of Eve is that of traditional art dressed up in modernity's artifices, and it is this revision of aesthetic tradition that the following study addresses.

Many of Villiers's texts depict ideal female protagonists; they include Elisabeth of *La Révolte*, Claire Lenoir of *Tribulat Bonhomet*, Tullia Fabriana of *Isis*, and Sara Maupers of *Axël*. All of these women are endowed with extraordinary physical beauty and equally astonishing intelligence and spirituality. The same is true of many of Villiers's male characters: Axël, Sergius d'Albamah of *Le Prétendant*, and Ewald, to name but a few. Yet when Villiers chose to create a completely artificial character who would be the consummate embodiment of these qualities he decided upon a *female* automaton. It is my contention that this choice is far from gratuitous. The birth of the modern artificial in the nineteenth century and concurrent discourses on the relationship between art and technology lend themselves quite predictably to a construction of the feminine. This study concentrates in particular on two technologies and arts – sculpture and photography – that act as veritable dynamos for the reproduction of this artificial feminine.

Whereas traditional critics, including A. W. Raitt, P.-G. Castex and Max Daireaux, have recognized *L'Eve future* as a significant nineteenth-century text, they have not considered at length the novel's sexual politics, that is, Villiers's rediscovery and recreation of a specifically female body. Post-structuralist critics have, on the other hand, brought to light the modernity of *L'Eve future*, the self-reflexive aspects of the text and the discourse on artificiality that it presents. In *Le Silence éloquent*, for example – the only book-length study of the novel to date – Deborah Conyngham exposes an oft-remarked parallel between the textual structure of *L'Eve future* and Edison's construction of Hadaly, a parallel that has been expanded on by Jean-Louis Schefer. Neither Conyngham nor Schefer devotes particular attention to the gender of this inscription, however.

Feminist and film theorists have realized the implications of this symmetry between the chapters of the text and Edison's verbal dissection of the specifically female body. Annette Michelson, one of several critics to have stressed the novel's relationship to the birth of the cinema, has described *L'Eve future*'s literal inscription of the female body in this way: "If . . . Miss Clary is but an empty vessel, Edison's text, whose complex articulations, fine tolerances, and inscriptions will fill that vessel, vivifies the statue's body, fragmenting, analyzing, then restoring, through inscription, this body" (18).

Michelson interprets Edison's words or the masculine power of speech as the clay or molten bronze that would complete the empty shell of woman. She refers here to the positivist's lecture on the topology of the female body: he orally exposes Hadaly to Ewald during an all-night discussion. The books and chapters of the text are thus mirrored by the limbs of Hadaly's body; there is indeed something peculiarly feminine about this text. Moreover, it is not surprising that *L'Eve future* is quickly becoming a major literary reference in discussions of the (especially early) cinematic portrayal of the female body. The brief passage in *L'Eve future* that stages the projection of woman by means of "successive photography" is the focus of much of the current attention given to the novel. Studies of this kind have also contributed to the vast and fertile discussions of gender and technology that feminist film theorists in particular have undertaken. Although fundamental, cinema is, however, only one of the technologies employed by Edison in his recreation of Eve, and is but one of the technologies addressed in this study.

Other postmodern and/or feminist critics who have participated in a revalorization of *L'Eve future* and specifically its female characters are Marie-Hélène Huet, who stresses the maternal and monstrous in *L'Eve future*; Rodolphe Gasché and Carol de Dobay Rifelj, who admirably decipher Hadaly's problematic identity; Linn B. Konrad, who has compared the android to several other Villierian heroines; and Jeffrey Wallen, who notes that "The one mark of difference . . . that seemingly continues to operate most strongly in the text is that of sexual difference" (39). *L'Eve future* would seem in fact to be on the tip of postmodernity's tongue; neglected in the past, it is quickly becoming – in these years surrounding the centennial of its publication – a privileged illustration of the representation of the feminine.[1] Naomi Schor's assertion that "Villiers de l'Isle-Adam's *l'Eve future* would [in a revamped canon] displace J.-K. Huysmans' *A Rebours* as the ultimate text of post-realism, for Villiers' futuristic fantasy of a female android is the logical conclusion of a century of fetishization of the female body" (*Breaking* 145-46) is not only the dream of every devotée of *L'Eve future*, but is indicative of the current urgency to understand such a rich text. In

---

[1] A major sign of a renewed interest in *L'Eve future* is the forthcoming collection of essays on the text edited by John Anzalone. I was not able to consult all of the essays before this book went to press.

order to further this fortunate recognition of *L'Eve future*, critical works that question Villiers's ideology of the feminine are needed. The novel must also be situated in a historical context, for only by reading *L'Eve future* as a product of nineteenth-century Europe's fabrication of woman can we trace its contribution to present-day discourse on the feminine.

The neglect of the feminocentric aspects of *L'Eve future*, of, in Pascal Rollet's words, "a resistant female voice in *L'Eve future*," has led to a neglect of the female creator of the text. Like Hadaly, Sowana the lab assistant appears rarely, and then often by surprise, during Edison's lengthy discussion with Ewald. All but mute, Sowana cannot define herself, nor is she defined satisfactorily by her "creators," Villiers and Edison. Like Hadaly, she remains a mystery, an incarnation of the enigma of femininity. Several critics have followed Villiers's lead and have passed over Sowana's significance with "explications rapides" – the title of one of *L'Eve future*'s chapters – that fail to satisfy. For example, Sowana has been presented as the scapegoat for the perplexing final pages of *L'Eve future* (Lebois, Konrad, Rose). This is to be expected and is perhaps a conscious move on Villiers's part, for, as Mary Ann Doane has pointed out in reference to science fiction, "A certain anxiety concerning the technological is often allayed by a displacement of this anxiety onto the figure of the woman or the idea of the feminine" ("Technophilia" 163). An important step toward deciphering the enigma of woman in *L'Eve future* is, therefore, the reproblematizing of the feminine as both *creator* and *creation* of art and science, as both *technical object* and *technology*, in the sense that she is an *object* projected by technicians and a *medium* that allows meaning to occur.[2]

The relationship of the female body to representation and the technological is currently being debated by feminists at the forefront of postmodern criticism. It has been shown for example that the "body politics" of science, especially in its technological and medical forms, has conspired to construct and deconstruct the female body as raw material for the fabrication of modernity's mores.

---

[2] I draw here on Friedrich A. Kittler's superb study, *Discourse Networks*. Kittler rightly identifies *L'Eve future* as a major literary instance of the "discourse network" (the notation system or technology of writing) that surrounds the year 1900.

Postmodernists are turning these mores inside out in an effort to benefit from modernity's emphasis on convention while at the same time avoid its restrictive and often colonialist views of what it is to be human. Villiers's novel is thus an extrememly significant "crossover" text, one that is eminently modernist – in its views of gender, the artificial and the machine, for example – but also fine food for thought in a postmodern era that can interpret in distinctive ways *L'Eve future*'s seemingly infinite *mise en abîme* of representation, gender, and the very question of what it means to be a "natural" body in a world overrun by simulation. In this sense, Villiers's text is a supreme example of how the postmodern may in fact be simply (but not too simply) another stage of modernism; *L'Eve future* encourages us to consider this possibility.[3]

One example of how postmodern theory can elucidate such a modernist novel is Donna Haraway's theory of the utopian body as cyborg, "By the late twentieth century, our time, a mythic time, we are all chimeras, theorized and fabricated hybrids of machine and organism; in short, we are cyborgs. The cyborg is our ontology; it gives us our politics" (174). Haraway's cyborg is a perfectly modern being who represents the breakdown of three traditional boundaries: that between the human and the animal; that between the organism and the machine; and that between the physical and the non-physical. In this new world order, Haraway continues, simulation replaces representation and replication takes the place of reproduction. This is the world order that such authors as Villiers romanticized and predicted. As Hadaly the "hybrid" slips freely across these borders and boundaries, she reveals the origins of this slippage in the nineteenth century's preoccupation with reproduction (of children), replication (of artworks) and the mechanics of the female body.

The current twentieth-century reign of technology that endows machines with representational and reproductive powers and relegates the feminine to the monstrous finds its source in the nineteenth century, that thermodynamic era that theorized and marketed an aesthetics of artifice. In order to understand the status of

---

[3] Andreas Huyssen is just one critic who has noted the "relational nature" of modernism and postmodernism: "Modernism as that from which postmodernism is breaking away remains inscribed into the very word with which we describe our distance from modernism" ("Mapping" 236).

women and images of women in our own mechanized and information-oriented society, it is therefore of the utmost importance that we inquire of poets and technology past, that we turn back to the primal fictional accounts of the very birth of the feminine as artificial. And certainly among these accounts, one must consider *L'Eve future*.

Chapter 1

REPRESENTATIONAL TEXTS

This chapter, a survey of nineteenth-century French texts that stage the recreation or representation of woman, is not an exhaustive review but rather an introduction to the theme that Villiers takes from his contemporaries and analyzes microscopically in his detail-rich narrative. Emphasized are those works that most succinctly address the fabrication of the feminine in its two major nineteenth-century modes: woman as technological innovation and woman as aesthetic masterpiece. Each of these modes of reproduction is given a crucial role in *L'Eve future*. The presentation of these glimpses of assembled and disassembled women will set the stage for a detailed investigation of Edison's android, who incarnates all aspects of the nineteenth-century ideal woman and foreshadows the fantastic females of an emerging era, our own.

These two generators of images, the technical object or machine and the aesthetic process, combine forces in the nineteenth century and promote a rejuvenated if not entirely new category, the artificial. Although the artificial certainly existed well before the last century, it was during the last fifty years of that century that it was fetishized in a particularly modern fashion. (A perfect example from Huysmans's *A Rebours* is des Esseintes's "visit" to London – he never actually leaves Paris.) The artifice that preoccupied the aristocratic dandy (and both Ewald and Villiers are dandies) set the parameters for two of his major paradoxes: while emulating the feminine, he rejected woman; while fetishizing the artifice of machines, he rejected the industrial age. These paradoxes are, *L'Eve future* shows, symbiotic. The artificial in the nineteenth century was indeed an ambivalent notion, combining as it did the age-old ability of art to *imitate* nature and the newly discovered, or at least newly imagined, ability of industry and technology to *replace* nature. And since "nature" had been aligned with "woman" at least since the beginning of the Romantic era, the artificial replacement of nature *naturally* entailed a replacement of woman. Two distinct currents in the literature of the time follow this bifurcation and *L'Eve future* heralds their synthesis.

The rather patchwork trajectory that follows is limited for the most part to short prose works, some well-known, others seldom-read. Taken together, they reveal a persistent inscription of the fragmented female body in nineteenth-century literature. Following an English prototype, *Frankenstein*, in which the female is torn literally limb from limb, these works dismember the feminine, reducing it to bits and pieces, and then reassemble it in a phantasmal ideal whole, itself broken down subsequently into its constituent parts. These odds and ends float through literary texts as signifiers – feet, hands, arms, breasts – unable for the most part to attach themselves to a transcendental signifier. For the image of woman that emerges from this piecemeal analysis is not one of transcendence, but of stark materialism, one that views woman as a privileged referent for artistic creation and a unique specimen for scientific exploration and technological innovation. The only transcendence obtained by the majority of artificial women in these texts is that of death.

Furthermore, the artists and scientists who fantasize such monstrous creations are quick to limit or deny their creations verbal powers and the ability to move. Like those female characters analyzed by Naomi Schor in *Breaking the Chain*, the products of the laboratory and the artist's studio are enchained – either within the confines of a frame or sculptural base, within the boxes and drawers that accompany the investigative process, or attached to the wires and electrodes of the laboratory. From *Frankenstein* to *L'Eve future* this process of confinement can be read as a history that slowly integrates technology into the aesthetics of the reproductive imperative. Villiers's female characters subvert this traditional enchainment, however – to what extent we shall see – and thus mark the end of an era.

[A] Bride of Frankenstein

Ellen Moers's compelling reading of *Frankenstein* (1818) as a birth myth is one reading that has brought to light the crucial influence of the maternal imagination on this apparently paternocentric story. Moers convincingly posits the text as a recognizably autobiographical work by relating Shelley's tragic loss of her own infants to Dr. Frankenstein's unsuccessful parenting of his monstrous progeny. According to Moers, the scientist, suffering from "trauma of the afterbirth" (93) or postpartum depression, refuses to acknowledge his child. Aware of his creator's failings as a provider, Shelley's creature characterizes his neglected childhood in terms of an interrupted pregnancy, "I, the miserable and abandoned, am an abortion, to be spurned at, and kicked, and trampled on" (244). But, it should be noted, the male monster is *not* aborted. Although he is denied maternal care, he does attain the status of adulthood, due in part to his acquisition of language or access to a symbolic order. The monster is denied a name, but he is able to name the objects around him. He recounts his own story, which centers to a certain extent on his reading of literary texts including Plutarch's *Lives*, the *Sorrows of Werther* and *Paradise Lost*. Through his participation in this intertextual code, Doctor Frankenstein's son is established as a full-fledged literary character.

Shelley does begin to sketch another being who, unlike the male monster, is shunned prior to birth, a creature who remains fragmented and whose story is abruptly interrupted – a *female* monster. The true "abortion" of the text is this Eve whom Dr. Frankenstein only *partially* creates (and Moers only briefly mentions). Frankenstein does not merely refuse to create again. On a dismal and remote Scottish island, he begins to piece together a female who will fulfill the monster's requirements, "My companion must be of the same defects. This being you must create" (154). Although Victor proceeds in the same manner as with the male, he is filled with apprehension and disgust while assembling the female:

> It was, indeed, a filthy process in which I was engaged. During my first experiment, a kind of enthusiastic frenzy had blinded me to the horror of my employment; my mind was intently fixed on the consummation of my labour, and my eyes were shut to

the horror of my proceedings. But now I went to it in cold blood, and my heart often sickened at the work of my hands. (178)

Whereas the creation of the male was accompanied by excitement and enthusiasm, the birth of the "filthy" female gives rise to new horrors and more intense fears, "she might become ten thousand times more malignant than her mate, and delight, for its own sake, in murder and wretchedness" (181). Worse still, the female will make possible the generation of an entire new "race of devils" that the male alone cannot produce.

Overcome by terror, Dr. Frankenstein aborts his second creation, although his work "was already considerably advanced" (179). Moreover, he does not simply discontinue his work, he deliberately and violently destroys the female, "trembling with passion, [I] tore to pieces the thing on which I was engaged" (181). When the doctor returns to erase his tracks from the scene of the crime, he is confronted by the following sight, "The remains of the half-finished creature, whom I had destroyed, lay scattered on the floor, and I almost felt as if I had mangled the living flesh of a human being" (186). Frankenstein then rows the remains of his daughter, weighted down in a basket with stones, out to sea, where he hears the creature's first and last utterance, a stifled cry, "[I] cast my basket into the sea: I listened to the gurgling sound as it sunk, and then sailed away from the spot" (187). Shelley's charting of sexual difference in this myth of siblings and mates is clear: whereas the lone and thus childless male is afforded a life, albeit tragic, the female, site of reproduction, is destroyed prepartum.[1]

Despite its failed fabrication of the feminine, *Frankenstein* is the foremost ancestor of a series of texts that modify the creation of woman theme so as to accommodate scientific and technological discourse. This text by an English woman writer set a precedence for similar versions of the creation myth by French male authors of

---

[1] The feminist literature on *Frankenstein* is extensive. At least two post-Moers readings of *Frankenstein*, one by Barbara Johnson and another by Sandra M. Gilbert and Susan Gubar, emphasize the monstrosity of, respectively, female autobiography and female literary creativity. But again, neither study recognizes the significance of *Frankenstein*'s female progeny. Marie-Hélène Huet's few comments on the unborn female are enlightening; she notes that the scene of the extremely violent destruction of this being was suggested by Mary Shelley's husband (154-55).

the nineteenth century. By the end of the nineteenth century and through to the early twentieth century, scientific Eves would populate French literature – in *L'Eve future*, of course, and also in works by Jules Verne, Raymond Roussel, and Alfred Jarry.[2] One might even propose that Villiers's *L'Eve future* is a fin-de-siècle sequel to or rewriting of *Frankenstein*, with Hadaly as the female whom Dr. Frankenstein and Mary Shelley were unable to complete. The technological climate of the latter nineteenth century allowed the creation of an artificial female to proceed and even necessitated that the prototypic modern monster be female, given its equation of the artificial and the feminine.

One writer responsible for the creation of such a climate was Charles Cros, a poet, humorist, and inventor who deserves attention as a contemporary influence on Villiers.[3] Cros wrote several important treatises on color photography and has been credited in France with the invention of the phonograph. Like the fictive Edison, he was concerned with the recording or reconstruction of the human voice. His verses reflect a nineteenth-century desire to replicate the spoken word:

> As the features in cameos
> I desired that loved voices
> be a blessing kept forever
> and repeat the musical dream
> of the too brief hour.
> Time would flee. I subdue it.[4]

The recorded voice of the lover is also a privileged phenomenon in *L'Eve future*; the phonograph is one of several technologies that endow the mechanical woman with verisimilitude and enable her to endlessly reciprocate her male lover's version of the ideal relationship between the sexes.

Two of Cros's short works narrate the technological recreation or renovation of woman. *La Machine à changer le caractère des femmes* (*The Machine that would Change the Female Disposition*)

---

[2] Carrouges provides a survey of these texts.
[3] And has been cited as such in Lebois and in the notes to the Pléiade edition of Villiers's works. Contemporary assessments of Cros are few and far between and concern his poetry, whereas two short prose works are analyzed here.
[4] Quoted in Lebois 198. All translations of Cros are mine.

(1875), a farce worthy of Tabarin, begins with the introduction of a new invention, a contraption that transforms an argumentative woman into a tranquil wife, "One enters on the right . . . One exits on the left – or vice versa –, and the most wicked dispositions become the sweetest; the tigresses of Hyrcania become sheep-like beauties; the fiercest angels become affable demons . . ." (390-91). The machine employed is in reality a chamber in which a certain Viscount Perlegrise satisfies his lust with the thereafter tamed shrew. Frontin, Perlegrise's valet, and Anselme, the metamorphosed woman's husband – who believes that those in the chamber are merely drinking champagne – look on as the activity occurring in the chamber is measured by a manometer, "During this time, a manometer (!) suspended on the door of the booth flutters madly to the point where Anselme worries and asks if the machine is fatal to one's health – Never, replies Frontin . . ." (391). The manometer, an instrument for measuring the pressure of gases and vapors, hangs over the door of the chamber, doubling Poe's purloined letter (which Lacan has spied between the chimney's "legs" [*Ecrits* 1: 47]).

This instrument clearly represents technology's appropriation of the female interior (in particular her sexual organs), its gases and vapors exposed to the charlatan's audience. Cros's tale thus suggests an identification between woman – in this case her participation in the sexual act – and energy, that is between woman and disorder, if we are to follow Michel Serres's convincing discussion of literary references to the second law of thermodynamics or the law of entropy in *Feux et signaux de brume*. Cros's story is an example of the nineteenth-century literary text (the machine/chamber reads as a metaphor for the text) that functions as a system designed to measure and regulate female sexual energy.[5] The cuckolded Anselme is duped by a device that both defines and recreates the female. In the same way, Villiers's Lord Ewald is duped by the reality effects of Hadaly's electromagnetic motor, infinitely more complex than the manometer but based on the same principles of energy conservation and inevitable entropic fragmentation.

In another of Cros's tales, *La Science de l'amour* (*The Science of Love*) (1874), a young positivist undertakes "the scientific study of

---

[5] Schor shows that this concern with energy conservation structures the (especially realist) nineteenth-century work, ". . . I am led to conclude that the binding of female energy is one of (if not) the enabling conditions of the forward movement of the 'classical text'" (*Breaking* xi).

love" (224).[6] To this end, he lures the young Virginie away with him and subjects her to a series of examinations that would measure her love. As poetry seduces, so science deduces in this tale. Cros's dissection of the feminine requires many hidden instruments, including a thermometer, a cardiograph, gadgets for measuring weight and perspiration, a kissing-counter, an atmospheric meter, and a "vexation mechanism" for assessing the effects of absence and longing. Several of these instruments are placed on the female body itself – hidden within Virginie's clothing, they transform her into an experimental terrain. The data recorded by Cros's narrator will yield not only a formula for love, but one for the feminine itself, which becomes an analyzable composition of air, water, and heat. The scientist is a mere buffoon, however, who in the end is deceived by the woman whose emotions he had hoped to isolate and classify; she has cheated on him while he has grown to love her. Aware of his endeavors, she destroys his instruments in a defiant refusal to submit to the scientific method, "all in fact was smashed, crushed under her boot heels; the burned documents fluttered here and there like a swarm of moths" (233-34). Worst of all, his love has blinded him to his quest for knowledge, "To top it off, losing the occasion to record the analytical elements of such profound distress, of such a peculiar combination of violent sensations, I didn't think to apply the cardiograph to myself!" (234). Only too late does the scientist realize that he has been feminized and has become an appropriate specimen for his own experiment. In the end, however, woman does not escape confinement – Virginie flees in the trunk of her new lover.

These two texts fictionalize attempts to isolate, analyze, and classify the feminine, that is, subject it to the scientific method. Such endeavors point to an essentialist view of woman; although she may eventually – and will most likely – be labeled aberrant and readied for reconstruction, she is a phenomenon of nature and as such is quantitatively measurable and qualitatively assessable. The

---

[6] This text has been cited by many critics as a source of Villiers's short story *L'Appareil pour l'analyse chimique du dernier soupir* (*The Apparatus for Chemical Analysis of the Last Breath*) which appeared in 1874 under the title *L'Appareil du Docteur Abeille E.E. pour l'analyse chimique du dernier soupir*. In this story, included in the *Contes Cruels* (*Sardonic Tales*), Villiers imagines a gadget that measures the soul of a body *in extremis*. Moreover, Des Esseintes cites *La Science de l'amour* as the sole contemporary text that approximates Villiers's keen satire of modernity (Huysmans 325).

construction and destruction of woman undertaken by Shelley's natural philosopher requires a progressive containment of his specimen. Frankenstein fabricates the female in a small island hut/laboratory, then transports her to a rowboat, her remains gathered in a basket. Cros's chamber, with its signifying manometer, is a further instance of the sequestering of the feminine. Finally, in *La Science de l'amour* a clandestine *boudoir* serves as laboratory, while in *L'Eve future* Edison's laboratory is underground, accessible only by elevator.

The works of Jules Verne are saturated with machines that each obtain, in Jacques Noiray's words, "the status of a veritable fictional character" (37, trans. mine). Yet Vernian machines do not for the most part take on human form, as Compère has remarked (91). *Le Château des Carpathes* (*The Carpathian Castle*) (1892) is an exception; in this text, the image and voice of an ideal female character are mechanically recreated. The text stages a very literal isolation and replacement of the feminine. The Baron Rudolphe de Gortz returns to his long-abandoned Transylvanian castle with a portrait and phonograph recording of the Italian opera star who had enchanted his eyes and ears, La Stilla. Having accepted the Count Franz de Télek's marriage proposal, La Stilla collapses suddenly during her farewell performance in Naples, her untimely death provoked by Gortz's grotesque glance stalking her from a private theater loge – she dies of fright. Gortz has recorded her swan song and replays it, accompanied by the projection of her image, in the dungeon of his castle. His artificial world begins to collapse, however, when Télek, who wrongly suspects that Gortz has kidnapped the living Stilla, storms the castle and provokes the destruction of Gortz's creation. His representation demolished, Gortz triggers an explosion that levels the castle.

Gortz's representation of the feminine is twofold; both La Stilla's image and voice are isolated in mechanical "condensateurs d'Idéal" (Noiray 179), and then projected and amplified. The female voice is captured in an ornamental box: "Near the chair was a small cloth-covered table, and upon this was a rectangular box. This box, twelve or fifteen inches long and five or six wide, and whose raised cover was encrusted with jewels, contained a metallic cylinder" (178). The phonograph, invented by Edison (or Cros in some versions), is hidden in this jeweled case, reminiscent of eighteenth-century *serinettes*. Gortz controls this equipment and activates it when La Stilla's image appears. Although he intentionally shatters the singer's image (it is projected onto a glass screen), he retains her boxed song. Technology permits the possession of the female voice long after it has been disembodied, "But her voice – her voice shall stay with me! . . . Her voice is mine! . . . It is mine alone, and shall never belong to another" (181). Gortz owns La Stilla's sole access to the symbolic order, and nostalgically credits it with the power of presence – as Derrida has shown the voice to be traditionally endowed – although it in fact signifies a deadly absence. When the metallic cylinder, a version of Cros's manometer, is struck by a bullet, the Baron's experiment literally goes up in smoke. As Carrouges has pointed out, the female image/voice is a delaying device in *Le Château des Carpathes*; the end of La Stilla's song signals the end of both experimentation and representation, for they are one and the same thing. Her voice is shattered ("brisée") like a fallen laboratory flask containing the absolute feminine.

One means of interpreting the significance of Gortz's box is to label it a Freudian casket. In *The Theme of the Three Caskets* Freud states, in reference to Shakespeare, "If what we were concerned with were a dream, it would occur to us at once that caskets are also women, symbols of what is essential in woman, and therefore of a woman herself – like coffers, boxes, cases, baskets, and so on" (12: 292). Freud identifies the desirable casket/woman as the lead one, beautiful and deadly *silent*. Gortz's enclosure of the female voice would apparently subvert this interpretation. La Stilla's song is, however, devoid of presence and meaning, except in its reference to death; the only words that she sings are *"voglio morire."* [7] The phonograph box is, furthermore, shattered by a (lead) bullet. Gortz's fascination with the female box reveals, then, his own castration, which he would repair by stealing the female object. His perversion reveals in turn a desire to be "boxed in" (in his theater loge and his curtained armchair), in imitation of the feminine.

Gortz is not a scientist, but his companion Orfanik is a technician/inventor and predecessor of the Igor of cinematic renditions of *Frankenstein*. Verne's creation, like that of Villiers, is, however, much more than a technological construction. What distinguishes

---

[7] On this point, see Inez Hedges's study.

both La Stilla and Hadaly from mechanical contrivances and laboratory specimens is their status as *images*. The technical character of the female creation is implicated in a politics of plastic representation. Verne's audio-visual effects do allow his characters to transform the world, but more importantly, they reinforce a certain *image* of the world (in this case an image of woman), as Milner points out (233). This "imaging" of woman is yet another means of isolating and containing the feminine. The *parerga* of aesthetic representation – the painter's frame, the sculptor's base – are the artist's tools of confinement. And although the animated image often appropriates the power of movement, it remains nevertheless subject to severe restrictions governing the represented feminine.

[B] CHEFS-D'OEUVRE

Nineteenth-century French texts that stage the reinvention of woman as plastic representation are plentiful, due in part to a "Pygmalion complex" that afflicts Gautier's protagonists as well as many others of the literature of the time.[8] In *Laocoön*, Lessing had strictly limited painting to the representation of bodies side by side in space; this he opposed to the function of poetry which was to articulate sounds or actions successively in time. In nineteenth-century literature, painting (and to a lesser degree, sculpture) appropriates the power of poetry and evokes the fluidity of both time and space. Oftentimes, painting itself borrows from sculpture in animating the static portrait in three dimensions. Due to this Pygmalion obsession, *L'Eve future* represents a culmination not only of *Frankenstein*'s scientific construction of woman, but also of the fantasy of the animated artwork as ideal female.[9]

Pliny the Elder has left us with an anecdote cited in numerous queries of the limits of realist representation that admirably sums up the fundamental problematic of representation. His account of

---

[8] I borrow this phrase from Ross Chambers ("Gautier").

[9] There is no series of nineteenth-century French texts that portray the animation of the photographic image. This lack is surprising, given the significant influence exerted by the camera on mid to latter-nineteenth-century society. Photography cannot, of course, be neatly appended to painting, but it does belong to a similar tradition of two-dimensional representation. One of Villiers's innovations is, precisely, the choice of photography as a tool for the creation of the ideal feminine.

the competition between two painters, Zeuxis and Parrhasios, ends with Zeuxis's success in fooling birds with a depiction of grapes, whereas Parrhasios deceives his friend with a painted veil so lifelike that it induces Zeuxis to look behind it. Jacques Lacan's interpretation of the tale, useful in a discussion of artifice, hinges not on Parrhasios's painterly dexterity but on his choice of the veil as subject matter, "the [opposite] example of Parrhasios makes it clear that if one wishes to deceive a man, what one presents to him is the painting of a veil, that is to say, something that incites him to ask what is behind it" (*Four* 112). Zeuxis's fruit is "for the birds," it is a lure, a mere illusion, or that which deceives in nature. Parrhasios's veil, on the other hand, is a *trompe-l'oeil* that, one may infer, aims beyond the satisfaction of need (*besoin*) and demand (*demande*) to operate in the register of desire.

Lacan identifies the *trompe-l'oeil* with his *objet petit 'a'*, the Freudian fetish or that which substitutes for the al*lure* of the mother's phallus. The fetish/veil/*trompe-l'oeil* covers the original absence of the m(Other), that "hole" that all painting is doomed to expose:

> Indeed, there is something whose absence can always be observed in a picture – which is not the case in perception. This is the central field, where the separating power of the eye is exercised to the maximum in vision. In every picture, this central field cannot but be absent, and replaced by a hole – a reflection, in short, of the pupil behind which is situated the gaze. (*Four* 108)

The veil is constructed as an eyelid to dissimulate direct (eye)contact between this "champ central" (woman's hole) and the *regard*, or masculine gaze, that peeks out from behind the portrait. This Peeping Tom, if the veil is removed, finds himself confronted with his own castration, "in the scopic field, the gaze is outside, I am looked at, that is to say, I am a picture" (106). The veil becomes a screen that elides the subject (108). In short, Lacan is asserting, although perhaps unwillingly, that phenomenon noted by Kaja Silverman concerning the cinematic image: the image (or projection) stands not for a female lack, but for a masculine absence (*Acoustic* 30). Lacan's "pupil behind which is situated the gaze" would spy a castrated male spectator, that is, no one at all.

The construction of the female image in *Le Château des Carpathes* is an exemplary illustration of the Lacanian veil. In Gortz's dungeon peep show, the fetishist's desire is mediated by two screens: the Baron sits before a curtained stage and behind a screen, "About ten feet from this platform, from which it was separated by a breast-high screen, was an antique, tall-backed armchair, lit but dimly because of the screen" (177-78). Gortz recreates here (in a "screened" memory) the *trompe-l'oeil* of the primal scene that he had fabricated in his private grilled theater box. On the one occasion when he lowered the grille, Gortz's Medusa glance (in a reversal of gender roles) killed the woman. Gortz castrates La Stilla, who until this moment had refused to look at (to desire) her spectators, "Never had she loved, never had her eyes responded to the thousand looks which were concentrated on her upon the stage. It seemed that she lived for her art and for her art alone" (109). La Stilla is punished by the silent Gortz, who appropriates her voice. Gortz then resumes his role as Perseus when he constructs the veil (shield) which allows him to contemplate only the *image* of woman.

Gortz, who retains the authority of the gaze, is able for one moment to pass beyond the screen of representation, in a murderous move. La Stilla, however, is maintained as an image who is unable to cross to the other side of the kind of wonderland mirror theorized by Luce Irigaray, "How can I be distinguished from her [Alice]? Only if I keep on pushing through to the other side, if I'm always *beyond*, because on this side of the screen of their projections, on this *plane* of their representations, I can't live. I'm stuck, paralyzed by all those images, words, fantasies. *Frozen*. Transfixed, including by their admiration, their praises, what they call their 'love'" (*This Sex* 17). This would be La Stilla's grievance if she could articulate it; paralyzed, frozen, she *is* not, she is *projected*. In conclusion, the veil of representation has been erected to (1.) protect man from woman's image, and (2.) deny woman access to her image and thus to a possible wholeness or identity. La Stilla deceased, Gortz carries her, his fetish-in-a-box, the sound barrier or veil of song that would protect him.[10]

---

[10] For more on *Le Château des Carpathes*, see Serres's reading of the text as an Orpheus myth in *Jouvences*, Mustière, Jacques Neefs, and Didier Coste. I have situated *L'Eve future* as a more modern version of the artificial feminine theme, since Verne's La Stilla is only reproduced in two dimensions. Franc Schuerewegen, however, argues in his reading that Verne goes farther than Villiers, since La Stilla is never actually developed as a living character and is thus *pure* image, "Thus, *Le Château des Carpathes* is perhaps the missing link between the slightly embarrassed technologism of Villiers, who foresees the perversion inherent in the teletechnical phenomenon but believes he can correct it by a metaphysical point of view, and the place that *télétechnè* will hold in twentieth-century literature" (50).

Renditions of Pygmalion's plight in nineteenth-century French literature revolve to a large extent around the frustrated attempts of the male spectator to cross just such a veil, screen, or distance separating him from the represented woman. Gortz's success ultimately leads to death, as do most similar endeavors. Honoré de Balzac has fictionalized many such fetishistic follies. In *Le Chef-d'oeuvre inconnu* (*The Unknown Masterpiece*) (1832; 1845), two painters persuade a third to expose his concealed masterpiece. The mere fact that Frenhofer has kept his *Belle Noiseuse* out of sight induces Poussin and Porbus, modern Zeuxises, to bargain for a glance at the painting. Their bargaining chip is Poussin's mistress and model, who will pose for the completion of the *Belle Noiseuse*. Thus the real woman is exchanged for the image, as Ewald will discard Alicia in favor of Hadaly. When Frenhofer unveils his work Poussin sees only a "wall" of paint, but a detail alerts Porbus to the woman beneath: "Approaching the painting, they saw, in a corner of the canvas, the tip of a naked foot, emerging from a chaos of colors, tones, nuances of life. It was a delicious foot! A living foot! . . . 'There's a woman underneath,' exclaimed Porbus" (51-52). The female foot, like the manometer, signifies female sexuality – explosive and uncontrollable, it emerges from the canvas although it is ultimately contained by the frame of representation.

This female fragment, shining through the veil, reveals the painting's status as a *trompe-l'oeil*. Frenhofer truly believes that his relationship to the *Belle Noiseuse* is that of lover to mistress, not painter to canvas. The portrait is a living woman, he insists, "You're looking for a painting, but you should be looking for a woman! . . . But look! She breathed. Her breast! It moved. Ah! Who would not adore her? Wait. I believe she is about to rise!" (50). The artist has endowed his painting with a soul and has fantasized her animation, but as with Doctor Frankenstein's creation, the doubts that the feminine inspires (translated by Frenhofer's oscillation between line and color) ultimately condemn his creation to a fragmentary and partial existence. And, as with Gortz and Ewald, death is Frenhofer's sole escape from such a monstrous, albeit ideal, representation.[11]

---

[11] For more on *Le Chef-d'oeuvre inconnu*, see Serres, *Genèse*, Hubert Damisch, Jean-Luc Filoche, and my article "Modesty and the Artist's Model in *Le Chef-d'oeuvre inconnu*."

Balzac's *Sarrasine* (1830) also stages the artist's quest for the absolute in a plastic representation of the feminine. La Zambinella, the masquerading opera star of this tale, belongs to that category of female performers that populates nineteenth-century French literature and includes La Stilla, Alicia Clary, and Evelyn Habal. The reader is introduced to La Zambinella through works of art, first in a painting by Vien that inspires Girodet's *Endymion* and then in a statue by Sarrasine from which Vien's painting is drawn. This passage of the (fe)male from statue to painting signals, Roland Barthes notes, a progressive containment:

> Sarrasine dead, La Zambinella emigrates from statue to canvas: something dangerous has been contained, exorcised, pacified. In passing from volume to plane surface, the copy loses or at least attenuates the burning problematics the story has continually evoked . . . Passed down along the duplicative chain in the paintings of Vien and Girodet, the sinister story of La Zambinella grows distant, no longer exists save as a vague, moon-struck enigma, mysterious without being offensive . . . (*S/Z* 207-08)

The existence of multiple plastic copies of La Zambinella negates her/his power or authority as a masterpiece fetish. Moreover, the literary representation of La Zambinella boxes her/him in once and for all. Furthermore, the progression from statue to painting to written text is, it should be emphasized, accompanied by La Zambinella's transformation from female to male. Whereas the statue is an original representation of woman, the two copies are second-hand renditions of the man. The female image has once again been quieted through replication – whereas the male masterpiece circulates freely in the text – putting an end to the monstrous reproduction of the feminine, as La Zambinella takes his place as a "man." Ultimately, however, when Sarrasine dies, so does his creation of woman.

Sarrasine is a fetishist whose collection of *objets 'a'* is vast: the artist admires La Zambinella's legs, breasts, shoulders, neck, hands, and knees. An idealist, he assembles the female body parts in a harmonious whole, a bound "dictionary of fetish objects" in Barthes's words (*S/Z* 112). Moreover, La Zambinella's own body constitutes a *trompe-l'oeil*, as the spectator/reader both sees and does not see her/his castration. Like Frenhofer, Sarrasine fails in his depiction, codification, and containment of woman precisely because the central field (*champs central*) behind the veil is a blind spot, a locus of doubt that leads the artist to destroy his representation of woman (Frenhofer burns his canvas; Sarrasine believes that his hammer has demolished the statue), as Frankenstein tears his daughter into fragments.

The setting for many of Théophile Gautier's texts is, one might say, a museum of animated artworks representing the feminine. In *Mademoiselle de Maupin* (1835), paradise is described as consisting of "objects to be admired [*des machines à plaisir*], pictures which have no need of a frame, statues which come to you when you call them and wish to look at them closely" (142). Machines, paintings, statues, this is the associative chain of living images that the novel's main character, d'Albert, fantasizes. These ideal projections are, needless to say, feminine artifices; Gautier's protagonist is describing a harem ("ce sérail fantastique") of plastic female specimens from all parts of the world. Likewise, many of Gautier's short stories recount the adventures of an animated work of art or bibelot. *Omphale, histoire rococo* (*Omphale, A Rococo Tale*) (1834) is a humorous account of a tapestry figure come to life, and *La Cafetière* (*The Coffee-Pot*) (1831) allows its narrator to dance with an animated ivory woman who is subsequently frozen back into her form as a coffee-pot and then shattered on the floor.

In *Le Pied de momie* (*The Mummy's Foot*) (1840), "pédophile Gautier"[12] endows his narrator with Frenhofer's fetish, and has him purchase a paperweight in the form of a female foot. The protagonist first believes this fragment to be that of a Venus statue, but soon learns that it is the preserved foot of an Egyptian princess. This princess, Hermonthis, arrives in the narrator's bedroom and demands the return of her embalmed appendage. Her foot reattached, she takes him on a journey to ancient Egypt, where the young man (who has fallen in love with his mummy) asks the pharoah for Hermonthis's hand in marriage since "her hand for her foot seemed an antithetical compensation of quite good taste" (*Récits* 192, trans. mine). The pharaoh refuses and the narrator awakes in nineteenth-century France with a statuette of Isis (recalling the

---

[12] I borrow Sima Godfrey's coinage. Godfrey reads the sexually potent foot image as a metaphor for artistic or writerly competence. Her study draws on Jean Bellemin-Noël's fundamental structuralist analysis of Gautier's fantastic texts, "Notes sur le fantastique."

fragmented Osiris) to replace his lover's foot. Her tomb ransacked by a greedy and jealous dealer in bric-a-brac, the princess had lost her phallic attribute in the disassembling of antique masterpieces or mummies that occupied archaeologists and historians of Gautier's time. This tale humorously fictionalizes the consequent passage of woman from fragmented body to fragmented and abstract *objet d'art* (from foot to hand to bibelot).

Le Pied de momie resembles two other texts by Gautier, *Le Roman de la momie* (*The Romance of the Mummy*) (1857) and *Arria Marcella, souvenir de Pompéi* (*Arria Marcella, Pompeiian Souvenir*) (1852), in its choice of an ancient empire as the setting for the reanimation of a woman who has been "killed into art."[13] This passage from dead *oeuvre* to living woman hinges on what Gautier calls "retrospective love," that is, love that defies the limits of time and space. Retrospection is a phenomenon fictionalized in many texts of the time including *L'Eve future*, in which Edison imagines visiting Babylon, Alexandria and Greece in a chapter called "Rétrospectivité," and in which Ewald has just returned from Abyssinia. Chambers has convincingly related this preoccupation with past civilizations to the disorder and fragmentation of a modern world afflicted with entropy ("Gautier" 641-42). As already noted, this evidence of the laws of thermodynamics is often displaced onto the female body in the literature of the time. The ancient ruins uncovered in the eighteenth and nineteenth centuries warned of the perishable nature of culture, which survives only in bits and pieces: these are often the bits and pieces of the female body, her hands, feet, neck, breasts, etc. The task of the scientist, artist, archaeologist, museum curator, and poet was to classify, organize, and assemble in a harmonic whole these scattered fragments. Ideal woman, for Gautier, is a reconstructed *monceau* of *morceaux*, a pile of pieces.

In *Le Roman de la momie*, an extended version of *Le Pied de momie*, Lord Evandale (a precursor of Ewald) falls in love with a mummy during an archaeological expedition. Again, the mummy appears as an exotic variation on the Venus statue: Queen Tahoser poses in her mummified state as the *Medici Venus*. Octavien, the hero of *Arria Marcella* and also a victim of retrospective love, falls

---

[13] In their analysis of the female image (in this case woman's image of herself), Gilbert and Gubar borrow this phrase from Wolfgang Lederer, who asserts that women apply the death mask of makeup in order to attract men (14-15).

for a stone artifact, a specimen in the Naples Museum archeology collection:

> The thing that he was examining so closely was a piece of coagulated black ashes, bearing a sunken impression; one would have said that it was a fragment of a statue mould, broken in its casting; the trained eye of an artist would easily have recognized the curve of an admirable breast and a flank as pure in style as that of a Greek statue. (*Récits* 237, trans. mine)

Octavien had always dreamed of romancing the stone, "Sometimes, too, he loved statues, and one day, while passing before the *Venus of Milo* at the Museum, he cried out to himself: 'Oh! who will return your arms so that you might crush me against your marble breast!'" (251, trans. mine; this is also Lord Ewald's dream). Transported back to Pompeii, his fantasy is realized as Arria Marcella holds him "in her beautiful statue's arms, as cold, hard and rigid as marble" (269, trans. mine). As in *Le Pied de momie*, however, the young woman's father interrupts the romance and reestablishes the Oedipal triangle – mummy, daddy, daughter – that excludes the intruder/groom/archaeologist.

Prosper Mérimée's *La Vénus d'Ille* (*The Venus of Ille*) (1837) is yet another tale of archaeological love.[14] The narrator, an antiquarian and archaeologist, is a Parisian who has arrived in the remote provincial village of Ille to examine Roman ruins; his goal is to classify these fragments and transport them to a museum. Soon enough M. Peyrehorade – the narrator's host – unveils his latest find, a bronze Venus statue that will be responsible for the events that occur on the wedding day of M. Peyrehorade's son, events that cannot be explained scientifically and that leave the narrator perplexed. The young Peyrehorade has placed his bride's wedding band on a finger of the *Venus* during a game of *jeu de paume*, but, unable to remove it, he must give his bride a different ring. The next morning the groom is found dead in his nuptial bed, "One

---

[14] Resemblances between *Arria Marcella*, *La Vénus d'Ille*, and Wilhelm Jensen's *Gradiva* (1903) are noteworthy. Jean-Luc Steinmetz holds that Freud's reading of *Gradiva* in *Delusions and Dreams* is in fact an analysis of Gautier's text by way of Jensen, who has introduced the notion of the unconscious in his "sequel." *Arria Marcella* emerges, then, as a privileged instance in psychoanalytic discourse on art. See also Luciana Grasso's article on this subject.

would have said that he had been squeezed by an iron ring" (238). His bride, who has gone mad, accuses the statue of murder. The narrator leaves the region dumbfounded; he even declines to divulge his original desire concerning the statue to his mourning host. Finally, the statue, which had already been an object of fear in the village, is melted into a church bell.

The *Venus* animated by Mérimée represents the cruelty and revenge suggested by her inscription, *Cave Amantem* (beware of love). Serres points out the common Latin origin of *statue* and *victim*, which both signify *substitution* ("Un Dieu" 18). The *quasi-objet* that is the bronze *Venus* belongs to a metaphoric chain of substitutions that includes the *jeu de paume* ball, the wall, two wedding bands, and the church bell. The female statue, a victim of "lapidation," victimizes the town of Ille and in particular the young Peyrehorade, who dies (is mummified) in her embrace. Serres's *quasi-objets* establish, he asserts, the circulation that composes the social order, represented by the ball that is passed from player to player. I would maintain, however, that *La Vénus d'Ille*, while revealing this passage, also denies it in a fundamental way. M. Peyrehorade's animation of the statue and the narrator's desire to freeze it as a work of art would force the *Venus* to participate in the commodity circuit or economic order of the art market. In a rush to recreate the ancient female ideal, nineteenth-century archaeologists assembled representative pieces as objects of the museum spectator's gaze. This fictional statue lashes out to castrate the male spectator by refusing to circulate as such an object before the visitor to the museum/mausoleum that would contain her. A *trouvaille* (find), she violently denies her status as *trou* (hole), preferring to remain underground as a whole and unexposed mummy. *La Vénus d'Ille* is, then, a very modern interpretation of the traditional myth of the animated and vengeful Venus statue, and its narrator represents the incursion of the museum and art market into this tale.

Villiers himself authored several works, collected in the *Contes cruels* (*Sardonic Tales*), that foreshadow *L'Eve future* in their paradoxical assessment of modern love and the influence of technology on conceptions of artifice, sincerity, and desire. *L'Appareil pour l'analyse chimique du dernier soupir* (*The Apparatus for Chemical Analysis of the Last Breath*) draws its subject, the containment of the essence of a human life, from Cros's *La Science de l'amour*. *L'Affichage céleste* (*Celestial Advertising*) (1875) concerns another modern invention, an advanced system of publicity that will announce such feats as the multiple reproduction of sculptures. Furthermore, two of the stories predict Villiers's own eventual recreation of Eve. In *La Machine à gloire* (*The Glory Machine*) (1875), several *andréides* serve as artificial clappers in theater audiences in order to influence the public's reaction to certain performances, and in *Le Traitement du docteur Tristan* (*Doctor Tristan's Treatment*) (1877), Edison's "Eve nouvelle" is mentioned as an instigator of love. Finally, *L'Inconnue* (*The Unknown Woman*) (1876) stages the love of a disillusioned aristocrat for an ideal who vanishes like the diva who has performed her swan song. The themes of sincerity and repetition and their relationship to effective communication are explored in this prelude to Ewald's romance with Hadaly. Already, therefore, Villiers had saturated the contemporary journals that published these stories with tales of mechanical devices, technical masterpieces labeled as female, and the doomed love affairs of the modern world.

L'Eve future is startling in its dramatic departure from these fragmentary readings (or writings) of the feminine. In a text that situates the artificial woman as both a work of art and a technical object, Villiers (Edison, Lord Ewald, and Sowana) succeeds in giving birth to a complete and unique being. Hadaly's stance as an active character who operates beyond male desire is a crucial twist to the discourse on the representation of woman that earlier fictions put forth. The novel remains, however, entrenched in a tradition that sets forth the laws governing the representation and construction of the feminine, and the bulk of the text depicts an assemblage of woman from her fetishized body parts. Hadaly, too, suffers in the end the containment and death of the fabricated female. *L'Eve future* is on the one hand an all-encompassing summary of an entire century worth of the fracturing of woman, and on the other, an apparent assertion that the sum of woman is indeed greater than the parts. In the end, the familiar problematic of the representation of woman is not resolved in *L'Eve future* – far from it, for Edison's decision not to fabricate future female androids is a reinforcement of the doubt that the female image projects. The nineteenth-century reader had in fact come full circle, for Edison's refusal eerily echoes Frankenstein's vehement "no." With a difference, however. This difference, which emerges from the pages of Villiers's humorous, absorbing, troubling, and often frustrating text, is what I mean to disentangle in the chapters that follow.

CHAPTER 2

PHOTOSCULPTURE [1]

In book 5 of *L'Eve future,* Edison, having convinced Ewald of the desirability of creating an artificial female, enters into an explanation of the feasibility of such an endeavor. To do so, he first opens Hadaly's armor to reveal her interior; he will then examine her exterior. In beginning such a journey into the interior of the android, Edison and Ewald blatantly disregard her warning concerning the danger of knowing all her mechanical secrets. Hadaly cautions Ewald against the discussion/dissection of the artificial when she says in reference to her nightingale's voice, "you must admire it; but don't try to understand how it is produced . . . God would withdraw from the song!" (95, 873).[2] The novel is, then, more than the Faustian blasphemy against God that traditional critics have called it; it is a willful violation of the female body despite its subject's admonition. Towards the end of the novel, Ewald will relinquish this need to comprehend the particulars of the feminine, "I personally believe that Hadaly is a true phantom, and I have no wish to explain or explore the mystery animating her. I hope soon to forget the little you've taught me on the subject" (206, 1000). Once Hadaly has assured Ewald that she will fulfill his desire by reflecting him faithfully, Ewald sees no need to pursue his investigation of her physical being. Edison has taught him far more than a

---

[1] A slightly different version of this chapter has been published in the *Australian Journal of French Studies* with the title "Snapshots of a Future Eden" and with accompanying illustrations from Gautier's pamphlet on photosculpture.

[2] First page references are to Robert Martin Adams's translation and second references are to the first volume of the Gallimard (Pléiade) edition of Villiers's works. Marilyn Gaddis Rose has also translated *L'Eve future.*

"little," however, for the majority of the text is devoted to the verbal fabrication of the android's armor and organs.

Edison's physical stance as orator and dissector during the first segment of his lecture is notable. In this scene as in many others, Villiers incorporates the performing and fine arts into his construction of the new Eve. Like Evelyn Habal's *danse macabre*, the drama enacted here is a morbid one: Edison the director/dissector proclaims his knowledge of the female corpse (the exposition of Hadaly is an "autopsy") to an audience of one: "The electrician stooped and loosened two steel clamps riveted to the floor, slid them beneath the feet of Hadaly, and then moved the table back to its horizontal position, with the Android now lying on it like a corpse on the dissecting table in an amphitheater" (125, 907). Standing thus, Edison recalls J.-M. Charcot, the nineteenth-century French neurologist who regularly exhibited his female patients before male spectators. Charcot's paralyzed and petrified hysteric is here replaced by another example of the feminine as artificial death: the sleeping beauty Hadaly is laid out on a stone slab and tinkered with by the scientist (and "prince") who will eventually awaken her.

Whereas Charcot's lessons were captured in photographs, Edison likens his own questioning of the sphinx to a painting, as he tells Ewald, "Think of the picture of Andreas Vesalius . . . Though we're alone down here, we're imitating the general idea of it at this moment" (125, 907). A painting of Vesalius, an anatomist who advocated dissection, standing before a rigid and exposed cadaver suggests the stiffness of the stone (dead) woman. During the analysis of Hadaly's interior, Edison dismisses Ewald's disgust with another allusion to dissection, "Is a doctor upset by what lies on a dissecting table when he's giving an anatomy lesson?" (161, 948). The most serious horrors of dissection – the liquids and odors of the corpse – are, of course, absent here. The knowledge that he is looking upon the interior of a possibly female being is, however, enough to disturb Ewald. One might say in fact that woman has been frozen here in a state of rigor mortis that resembles both Charcot's photographed hysteric in her trance and the solid state of the (Venus) statue. Technology has infused the *Venus de Milo* and given us a medico-aesthetic image of woman. Hadaly is waxen – she is a modern still life (*nature morte*) laid out on a (dissecting) table.[3]

---

[3] Annette Michelson has noted just such a relationship between a fascination

Briefly put, the medical technologies used by Edison allow the female organs to be displayed and ultimately reproduced, extending the containment and isolation of woman to include her *interior*.

The first term Edison uses to define his proposed separation of Alicia's body and soul is *transubstantiation*, that is, the transmutation of one substance into another. How the transubstantiation process is applied in the construction of Hadaly's exterior remains unclear, however. Much later in the text, Edison chooses to call the metamorphosis an "absolute transposition of the subject's appearance" (152, 936). This phrase is more precise, for Alicia does not literally transmute into Hadaly; rather, her form is copied onto the android's metallic skeleton. The central technique employed in this cloning of the real woman is photosculpture, a process that combines the reproductive potentials of the ancient art of sculpture and the novel technique of photography. Hadaly is the result of the interaction of these dissimilar arts, one producing a three-dimensional figure and the other an image captured in two dimensions. The *andréide* herself will be a multi-dimensional work of art.

There are several allusions to the photosculpture technique in *L'Eve future*. The first mention of photosculpture occurs at the beginning of Edison's mapping of the android's exterior, after he has completed her dissection and effected the closure of her armor. At this point Hadaly leaves the room, for her presence is not required during the oral analysis of her exterior. Edison now turns to the third element of her physical being: her *carnation*, or artificial flesh, the production of which requires the use of photosculpture.[4] Edison assumes Ewald to possess a basic knowledge of the technique:

> You know the fabulous results obtained by photo sculpture. One can achieve an absolute transposition of the subject's appearance. I have new instruments, perfected to a miracle, which

---

with the dissection of the female body and the image of the sculpted Venus. The "Waxen Venus" she discusses is a modern medical sculpture that foreshadows the females represented in the wax museums of the nineteenth century.

[4] The android is divided into four systems, two interior and two exterior: (1.) an interior living system, described during her dissection; (2.) a "plastic mediator," her armor, not discussed in depth; (3.) her flesh [*carnation*], which "forms the traits and contours of the imitated body, with the particular and personal emanation of the body to be reproduced, the hollows and swellings of the bony structure and the musculature, the system of veins and arteries, the sexuality of the model, all the proportions of the body, and so forth" (129, 908); and (4.) an epidermis, giving color and expression, or individuality, to the android.

were designed years ago under my supervision. With their help we will be able to transfer the identical outlines, down to the very slightest and most gradual contours, down to a tenth of a millimeter! Miss Alicia Clary will thus be photosculpted directly onto Hadaly, that is, onto the first sketch, sensitized for that purpose, in which Hadaly will already have begun to take silent form. (152, 936)

Photosculpture is then mentioned just before Ewald's garden scene with Hadaly. When Ewald wonders if Edison's engineers have discovered the true end of their project, Edison reassures him that "They saw nothing in the whole operation but an experiment in photosculpture" (188, 978). Photosculpture is thus presented as a well-known and accepted technique of the time.

Prior to Edison's mention of photosculpture to Ewald, the scientist had alluded to the process in his description of Sowana's role in Hadaly's construction:

It's indispensable for this work that your beloved be nude, and she will have no other witness than this great artist, who never idealizes but copies exactly. In order to grasp the precise mathematical form of our living lady, she will begin by taking, very quickly, in response to my detailed instructions, and with instruments of the most absolute precision, measurements of the waist, height, bust, feet, hands, legs, arms, and face with all its features, as well as the weight of your young friend. It will be a matter of no more than half an hour. (151, 935)

These measurements constitute an important step in the photosculpture process. With this data and the aid of photography, Sowana will draw exact copies of Alicia's form and pass them to Edison. In the chapter "Explications rapides," Ewald, quoting Alicia, restates Sowana's tasks, "She only paused occasionally 'to scribble figures and draw lines on bits of paper which she immediately handed to you'" (208, 1002). Sowana measures and traces onto paper Alicia's form, gathering statistics for Edison's use. Moreover, Ewald, still citing Alicia, notes the presence of light (implying photography) during this process, "And all this while a long 'streak of fire,' focused on the nudity of the model, seemed to follow the icy hands of the artist 'as if she was drawing with light'" (208, 1002).

In this same chapter, Edison's hurried explanations include the description of his use of photosculpture to inscribe Alicia's recitations with their accompanying intonations, expressions, and movements, onto Hadaly's cylinder-motor:

> Meanwhile I, with a micrometer in my hand and my strongest magnifying glass in focus, devoted myself to chiseling on the android's central cylinder none but the perfectly coordinated movements, none but the most subtle glances and joyous or serious expressions of Alicia. (215, 1011)

This scene is confusing when read alongside previous mentions of photosculpture because a new element is added, Alicia's voice. Sowana and Edison are not only transposing their model's frozen image, they are using photosculpture to record successive movements prompted by her readings. The passage is clarified when compared with an earlier one: "[Edison is speaking] And since time is golden, you can rehearse for me various scenes from a number of new dramatic productions that I have on foot, even as Miss Anny Sowana . . . aided by my advice, sets to work on a statue of you" (176, 963). Since time is money for the capitalist inventor and since Alicia is already posing for her physical transposition, Edison simultaneously records her voice on a phonograph and "sculpts" her movements onto the cylinder-motor.

This passage, in which Edison plays the part of the sculptor, contradicts several instances in *L'Eve future* when the scientist himself refers to Sowana as the artist who will sculpt the android. One of these passages, during which Edison praises Sowana's talents, contains an unspecified reference to photosculpture:

> She is not only a supreme artist in marble and alabaster, but the speed of her execution is literally prodigious! She makes use of hitherto unknown techniques, of all the most recent discoveries. [*Elle procède par des moyens tout nouveaux! Une découverte récente . . .*] In three weeks she can reproduce magnificently, and with an exactness that's positively uncanny, any sort of figure, animal or human. (175, 962)[5]

---

[5] In a note to this passage in the Pléiade edition, P.-G. Castex and Alan Raitt suggest that Edison refers here to electrotyping (*la galvanoplastie*). While electrotyping would fit in nicely with other technical processes mentioned in *L'Eve future*, it appears that this particular passage is a restatement of those concerning photosculpture. Certain words echo these other references, "all the most recent

Apparently, both Edison and Sowana, Hadaly's "parents," chip away at the blocks that compose the android.

Photosculpture is not one of Villiers's fanciful inventions. Invented in 1861 by a certain Willème, it belongs to a group of technologies that emerged in the late nineteenth century – the age of mechanical reproduction, to use Benjamin's phrase – and whose function it was to mass-produce statues and statuettes. As described in the article "La Photosculpture" in Pierre Larousse's *Grand dictionnaire* of 1874, the process requires the participation of five workers, both artists and technicians: a sculptor, a photographer, a draughtsman, a machinist (who may also be a sculptor), and an assistant machinist. As the *Grand dictionnaire* notes, photosculpture has "the appearance of a scientific, artistic, and industrial process." The complicated procedure can be summed up in three steps:

(1.) The model (plastic or living) poses on a base divided from its circumference into twenty-four equal parts. These sections correspond to twenty-four lenses that project from a circular darkroom surrounding the model. Once the latter poses or is posed, the sculptor activates the lighting mechanism that fixes the negative images onto glass proofs. In the hidden darkroom, the photographer develops these photographs.

(2.) The draughtsman transfers the twenty-four images onto paper by tracing them from an enlarged projection of each negative. Each detailed drawing is twice the size of the final product. The draughtsman's work also incorporates data gathered from a sphere suspended over the model that determines the relationship of each fragment to the base, establishing the model's vertical line.

(3.) Finally, a machinist copies each drawing onto a block of plastic material using a pantograph. The pantograph consists of two connected needles: one follows the drawing – attached to a wooden board – and the other chips away at the block, itself attached to a base again divided into twenty-four parts. The pantographer's chief function is to ensure the numerical correspondence of the drawings and the sections of the block. The assistant follows the lines of the

---

discoveries [*Une découverte récente*]" refers to Edison's new photosculpture tools, and the time period of three weeks is repeated soon after, in a reference to the sculpting scene (176, 963). From the beginning, Edison cites three weeks as the time needed to create Hadaly (53, 823). On the electrotype, see Beale.

sketch, while the pantographer guides the needle over the sculpture. A bit of retouching follows the procedure, as the lines separating the fragments are glossed over. A flattening technique (*l'aplatissement*) endows the final product with relief.[6]

The Larousse article strongly criticizes the results of photosculpture; they are faulty works, "vulgar and mediocre." Several reasons for Willème's failure are proposed; most of these involve photography's ineffectual translation of the model's three-dimensionality. Photography captures mere appearances, not reality, and thus allows for interpretation on the part of the draughtsman:

> Now, everyone knows that the lens works in optics as one eye alone, and that one eye can never perceive the true diameter of a cylinder, that it only sees the apparent diameter, which is as far from the real diameter as the observer is close to the object; it follows from this absolute and incontestable law that the photographer has only taken twenty-four apparent diameters in his rotunda, but not one real one; consequently, the pantograph can only reproduce twenty-four errors.

In the case of Hadaly, twenty-four errors would surely produce a monstrous ideal. In conclusion, the author notes, "One thus sees why photosculpture . . . can only produce very imperfect results." The use of photography and of a draughtsman flaws a process that should be left, it may be assumed, to less complex machines.

In an article in the *Moniteur universel* devoted to photosculpture, Gautier is of the opposite opinion. The writer and critic compares photosculpture's unjust critical reception to that received by photography and lithography:

> The fear has been expressed that photosculpture harms statuary and lowers gradually the level of this beautiful art, by substituting a machine for man and a procedure for intelligence. Photog-

---

[6] The pantograph resembles other copying machines of the nineteenth century, notably the reducing machine (in particular the Collas version invented in 1836) and the pointing machine. Neither of these techniques uses photographs and drawings as their basis of operation; the machinist instead works directly from a bronze or plaster model (reducing), or a stone figure (pointing). Nevertheless, similarities exist between these procedures and the use of the pantograph in photosculpture. See Beale 47. Much has been written on Villiers's description of Hadaly as a "writing machine"; see Carrouges, and Anzalone, "Golden Cylinders."

raphy was also the object of very similar grievances, which are not any more just. Upon its invention, lithography itself was accused of killing engraving. This opinion is not our own. (*Photosculpture* 9)[7]

Flaubert notes in his *Dictionary of Received Ideas* that photography will dethrone painting, but photosculpture, Gautier argues, will not do the same to sculpture. In fact, he continues, the new technique allows for more exact work and unveils the ideal sooner than traditional methods:

> Let the artist consider photosculpture a rougher at his command, and let him finish in one hour the already perfect and seductive work of the ingenious machine that welcomes the sculptor respectfully, although it can do without him. So many measures to take, so much fastidious fumbling, so many after-the-fact corrections, so many hundreds of sittings are done away with by photosculpture ... (10)

This assessment of photosculpture's rapidity seems to contradict *L'Eve future*'s description of Sowana measuring, calculating, and correcting. Very little time is required, however, "It will be a matter of no more than half an hour" (151, 935). Photosculpture is a true shortcut to an ideal, one that, for Gautier, has lost its referent, "Without a model, without a miniature, a mechanical rougher has provided with impeccable exactitude a statue *whose original does not exist*" (9, emphasis added). Photosculpture is for this very reason the perfect tool for Edison's factory, as it would yield a proliferation of copies whose originals are anonymous. In the same way that the *Venus de Milo* is the work of an "unknown sculptor" – in *L'Eve future* a mysterious sculptress – so the product of photosculpture is denied an author. Photography, an art accessible to and authorized by all, defines it, "[Photosculpture offers art] this statuette that belongs to no sculptor and that only the sun may sign. If it is not a *chef-d'oeuvre*, it is at least a marvel!" (*Photosculpture* 11-12).

According to an advertisement at the back of Gautier's pamphlet, a forty centimeter statuette would cost 200 francs to reproduce, yielding a price of about 800 francs for the first android. Sub-

---

[7] This article was later a pamphlet from which I am quoting. Translations of this article and of the Larousse entry are my own.

sequent copies of the prototype would be even less expensive. As Gautier says, "the century, although extravagant, is economical. Pure Art seems expensive" (10). Edison's new tools distinguish his use of photosculpture from Willème's procedure, however. These "instruments of the most absolute precision" (151, 935) are most likely meant to counteract the subjective nature of the photographic image. Hadaly can therefore be the walking and talking ideal of a thrifty century.

Photosculpture attempts to include a new and much-debated art, photography, in the already accepted practice of replicating plastic art objects. Villiers's choice of photosculpture as a privileged technique in the fabrication of the ideal feminine is not surprising, given the emphasis placed on both sculpture and photography in *L'Eve future*. Hadaly is more than a clone of Alicia – she is the *Venus de Milo* animated and restored to her rightful place in an idealization of woman. As for photography, one wonders if the construction of Hadaly could proceed without the use of this technical art. Photography and variations on it allow Edison to examine two unacceptable representations of woman, Alicia (whose photograph is projected onto a screen) and Evelyn Habal (whose dual nature is revealed through "successive photography" or film), in order to establish the motive for his recreation of woman. Photosculpture synthesizes these two generators of the image – it captures the feminine for eternity while it points to the close interdependence of modern representations of woman and technology.

The android, representative of all women, arises from the projection of one woman pieced together by means of a double aesthetic process. Along with operatic theater, photography and sculpture dominate the text, as Villiers questions accepted notions of originality and reproduction. Whereas sculpture grounds the feminine in eternity, that is, in a history that in the text is traced to antiquity, photography would render the feminine immediate and present. The new art is suggestive of the present due to its novelty in the nineteenth century and because it instantly records an "objective" reality. Sculpture recalls the past and foretells the future – its history and concrete three-dimensionality endow it with characteristics of the eternal. Photography reduces the past and future to the bold presence of Barthes's "message sans code" ("Message"). The ideal feminine thus emerges in *L'Eve future* as a being who, in defying time, answers to Baudelaire's aesthetic ideal, "By 'modernity' I mean the ephemeral, the fugitive, the contingent, the half of art whose other half is the eternal and the immutable" (*Painter* 13). The love of the thoroughly modern woman is one of eternal renewal and everlasting immediacy, as Edison tells Ewald, "The Android, as we've said, is nothing but the first hours of love, immobilized, the hour of the Ideal made eternal prisoner" (135, 916). Hadaly is both ancient and modern, classical and Romantic, past and present, a superposition of contrasting images produced by photosculpture.

CHAPTER 3

SCULPTURE

Edison's zealous reconstruction of woman – his hurried remodeling of Eve as the centerpiece of a future paradise – recalls, peculiarly enough, the great metropolitan upheaval of Villiers's time, the reconstruction of Paris. Carried out by the Baron Haussmann, the "Haussmannization" of the French capital was concluded in less than twenty years beginning in the 1850s. Hadaly is, in a sense, the body of this Paris; refabricated in the New World's garden of technology and meant to be delivered to the Old World, she is a new modern Eve built on the ruins of an obsolete Eden. Whereas Emile Zola's Nana is the literary symbol of a decaying Paris, of the *chantiers* and demolished organs of the city that are the negative side effects of Haussmann's venture, Hadaly is the idealized final product: a composite of shiny metal parts functioning in harmony, the whole retouched with the intricate detail of sculptural ornamentation. The comparison of Nana's body to Paris, with her diseased organs representing its boulevards and *chantiers*, is explicitly developed in Zola's novel.[1] But Villiers's Hadaly is also a representative body of the polis, a body that encloses the modern city not as infected entrails but as spectacle of silver, gold, and iron, an ideal exterior that hides a full range of technical objects from the phonograph (the city's lungs) to electrical wires (its street lamps). And as Nana represents the streetwalker who roams Haussmann's boulevards, Hadaly incarnates that spectacle in the form of Evelyn Habal, one of the android's many roles. For Hadaly, like the *grand*

---

[1] And has been discussed by, for example, Charles Bernheimer. See also Warner's discussion of the Haussmannization of Paris.

magasin, offers *all* the amenities of the great modern city of woman. As the ultimate female corpus of the city of the future, Hadaly replaces Nana as a truly acceptable version of femininity.[2]

Hadaly's sculpted exterior is – like the skeleton of the modern city – the work of artists, industrial engineers, and technicians. Indeed, all the workers in Edison's underground city of Eden are themselves sculpting or sculpted figures. Sowana is referred to as a sculptress several times in the text (151, 175; 935, 961), Edison recalls a Syracusian medal (7, 768), and Ewald's features are of a "régularité grecque" (790, not translated in the English). Alicia maintains the most direct relationship to a sculpted image; she is compared twice to the *Vénus Anadyomène*, but most often she is presented as a double of the *Venus de Milo* (at least eight times). Moreover, Alicia carries the sign of the statue in the form of "a fan of ebony, its ribs decorated with black flowers. On the material of the fan is represented a statue . . ." (155, 941). Carried before her like a scarlet 'A,' the fan's image immediately alerts the reader to Alicia's status as a principal link in *L'Eve future*'s chain of stone images.

Hadaly assumes sculptural stances several times in the text. When Ewald sees his intended mate for the first time she is posing as an awakening Galatea, "After an instant of immobility, this mysterious being descended the single step of her platform and advanced toward the two spectators in all her disquieting beauty" (58, 828). Then, during the reconstruction and subsequent deconstruction of Evelyn Habal, the statuesque *andréide* – a futuristic Statue of Liberty – provides the necessary lighting, ". . . Hadaly raised her torch over her veiled head to illuminate the dark drawer, standing beside it like a statue at the side of a tomb" (119, 900).[3] Although

---

[2] The film *Metropolis* makes clear the relationship between the mechanical woman and the city of the future. Thea von Harbou, author of the novel on which the film is based, was influenced by *L'Eve future*. On *Metropolis*, see Huyssen, "The Vamp and the Machine."

[3] Hadaly's resemblance to the Statue of Liberty in this scene is startling. Still a being of drapery and armor and lacking a soul, she is a true "hollow icon," as Albert Boime has called the Statue of Liberty. Coincidentally, the French gift to the United States was inaugurated in 1886, the year of *L'Eve future*'s publication in book form. See Boime and especially his chapter "Excursions on the Statue of Liberty." As Hadaly will endlessly re-interpret Ewald's desires, so the female *Liberty* represents renewed political dreams. On the identification of Hadaly and the vessel, see Conyngham.

Hadaly is never explicitly compared to the *Venus de Milo*, she is associated several times with the stone ideal. An obvious connection between the two is Sowana, the "unknown" sculptor who replaces the author of the Greek statue and becomes his female counterpart in the modern world.

Just as Hadaly is hailed in *L'Eve future* as a re-discovered Eve, so a particular fascination with stone women appeared in the nineteenth century as antique examples of the ideal feminine were unearthed and (re)evaluated. In fact, *L'Eve future* can be read as a history of this revision, that is, as a commentary on the introduction of the antique ideal into modernity's technological constructions of woman.

[A] STATUES

Baudelaire's generally negative but ultimately ambivalent assessment of sculpture is a propitious starting point for a discussion of sculpture's role in Hadaly's construction, given the poet's position as precursor of a movement – the decadent school – that conceives of the feminine as an artificial product of modernity and woman as a by-product of cosmetics. Baudelaire's ambivalence toward the feminine and the modern is reflected in his views on sculpture and photography. The criticisms of sculpture found in his *Pourquoi la sculpture est ennuyeuse* (*Why Sculpture is Tiresome*) (1846) point to a hesitation before the art of sculpture that strikes at the very heart of the art's status as aesthetic phenomenon.

Baudelaire makes his personal preference for painting perfectly clear in this essay. The critic's aversion to statuary representation may be summed up in one sentence: Whereas painting is an art of reason, or spirit, sculpture is rooted in nature. A *"Carib* art," sculpture gives form to the fetishes of primitive peoples. Painting, on the other hand, informs the human intellect and requires a certain hermeneutic sophistication or "initiation," "We find, in fact, that all races bring real skill to the carving of fetishes long before they embark upon the art of painting, which is an art involving profound thought and one whose very enjoyment demands a particular initiation" (*Art in Paris* 111). In other words, whereas sculpture is apprehended by the senses, painting demands a developed awareness of an aesthetic code; as sculpture is to nature, so painting is to culture.

Baudelaire presents three specific criticisms of sculpture. First, the sculpted image requires the spectator to choose a point of view that will be at best arbitrary and at worst faulty in regard to the artist's intention, "It is in vain that the sculptor forces himself to take up a unique paint [*sic*] of view, for the spectator who moves around the figure can choose a hundred different points of view, except for the right one . . ." (111). A second objection concerns what Baudelaire calls sculpture's complementary status. Relative to painting and architecture, sculpture is in a subservient position; its principle *raison d'être* is the embellishment of these primal arts. Finally, contemporary nineteenth-century sculpture is saturated with details that render it puerile:

> As soon as sculpture consents to be seen close at hand, there are no childish trivialities which the sculptor will not dare, and which triumphantly outrun the fetish and the calumet. When it has become a drawing-room or a bedroom art, it is the cue for the Caribs of lace (like M. Gayrard), or for the Caribs of the wrinkle, the hair and the wart (like M. David) to put in an appearance. (112)

The painterly gaze cannot endure the inconvenience of viewing sculpture and the intelligent spectator is bored before the ornamental nature of this humble art. In short, it would appear that Baudelaire's annoyance stems from the overall feminine nature of sculpture as opposed to (masculine) painting. Sculpture may very well produce the fetishes (supplements to the maternal) of primitives and ornaments of modern interiors, but it cannot express the civilized ideals of society. Although there is a "peintre de la vie moderne," there will be no sculptor of modern life.

Baudelaire is certainly not alone in subordinating sculpture to painting. As Herbert Read has argued, "painterly prejudices" have long caused artists and spectators to view (or read) sculpture as they would the painted canvas, in the end valorizing what we might call the more "reader-friendly" art of painting. Furthermore, an original identification between sculpture and architecture – ancient monuments are both buildings and sculptures – has obscured sculpture's potential as a unique art. Only since Rodin, Read argues, has sculpture begun to liberate itself from the visual and (re)discover its fundamental function as an expression of space through tactile sensation. Sculpture is at last free to fulfill its creative destiny, the "realization of an integral mass in actual space" (71). In addition, as feminist theorists have shown, Western civilization has historically privileged vision as the sense that most faithfully mediates experience and knowledge. A devalorization of the feminine, the material, the body, touch, taste, and sound – and perhaps sculpture itself – results from this reliance on the gaze as a means of recognizing and processing desire.

A certain historical valorization of painting at sculpture's expense is undoubtedly in large part responsible for the lack of theoretical literature concerning statuary art. An absence of discourse on the subject in turn reinforces sculpture's nebulous position, as Read points out, "Sculpture . . . has always had difficulty in establishing its independence as an art, and this has been in some measure due to the lack of any clear formulation of the requisite autonomous laws" (ix). Contemporary assessments of sculpture are scarce indeed, and it would appear that the statue has been denied a privileged place in the museum of contemporary debate.[4] This chapter sketches tentative topics for a needed debate on the relationship between narrative and sculpture and the status of the art as a privileged translator of the feminine. *L'Eve future* is an invaluable source for such a study, as it fictionalizes the birth of a statuesque Eve. The latter nineteenth-century liberation of sculpture encouraged the construction of a dynamic *Venus de Milo* and was in large part responsible for Villiers's choice of an animated statue as fictional character.

In studies of art in literature, painting again overshadows sculpture. There are, for example, numerous analyses of the painter in nineteenth-century literature, as well as of the relationship between painting and literature as arts.[5] Studies of sculptors and the significance of the sculpted object in literary texts of the time are scarce,

---

[4] Such diverse theorists as Barthes, Derrida, Lebensztejn, Lacan, and Damisch have written, some extensively, on the painted image and its status as text. Barthes, in *S/Z*, and Derrida, in *La Vérité en peinture* (*Truth in Painting*), do discuss sculpture, and their comments are illuminating. More often than not, however, sculpture appears as an appendage to their discourse on painting, with statues as the footnotes to the text of painting. Michel Serres's work has, however, brought sculpture into the forefront of contemporary thought.

[5] These include traditional studies by Fosca, Praz, Bowie, and Borowitz, and works influenced by contemporary theory by Steiner and Bal.

however. This is of course due in part to the more frequent appearance of the painter as fictional character; this imbalance itself indicates a possible hesitation before the representation of the sculptor. It would appear that the painter and canvas are deemed more representable, at least textually, than the sculptor and the carved image. Barthes's oft-cited identification of realist literature with the painting process in *S/Z* reinforces this nineteenth-century perception of literature as essentially a painterly activity.[6] This view in turn recalls Lebensztejn's recent theorization of the "readability" of the canvas – the two-dimensional painting is traditionally read from left to right and from top to bottom. The reading of sculpture may in time become thinkable as a result of postmodern literary texts that defy realist page constraints by promoting three-dimensional and non-linear reading, sometimes computer-aided. What is needed to further this potentially radical revision of our notion of the text are studies of literature and sculpture that valorize "sculptural reading." Until such work is done, we will continue to share Baudelaire's painterly prejudice.

Studies of the representation of women in stone and the relationship between sculpture and the feminine have also been eclipsed to a certain extent by studies of the painted woman. In fact, the sculptural representation of woman has been treated at length mostly in works on political or monumental sculpture.[7] The word "image" – in the process of being replaced by "text" – in contemporary readings of the social and psychological construction of the female body refers almost exclusively to painting and photography. And yet an entire history could be written on the dialogue between women and stone, a dialogue that continues to influence Western culture. From Galatea, who defied the laws of aesthetics to please her male lover/spectator, to the infamous Medusa, who usurped the power of the sculptor and froze her spectators solid,

---

[6] "Every literary description is a *view* . . . Thus, realism (badly named, at any rate often badly interpreted) consists not in copying the real but in copying a (depicted) copy of the real . . . " (*S/Z* 54-55). The painting in *Sarrasine* (and thus the literary text) is, however, dependent on an original statue. Sculpture is the first art to confine La Zambinella and the only one to represent (only) the masquerading female.

[7] See Agulhon, *Marianne*, and Warner. Warner's book does not deal exclusively with the sculptural. Serres's *Statues*, in turn, does not address the question of sexual difference.

mythical women have represented the metamorphic potential of marble and stone. Greek statues of Venus, Renaissance *Pietà*s, nineteenth-century monuments such as the Statue of Liberty, and twentieth-century renditions of the nude by Maillol and Moore continue to define the significance of the female body in society. Sculpture, which uncannily suggests the animate, is itself a dynamic cultural text. Furthermore, and perhaps to a greater extent than the canvas, the statue – in its three-dimensionality – confronts us with the *Other*, and it may well be in part this fear, the fear of the Other, that has caused a neglect of the sculpted image. Following Baudelaire (and Sherry Ortner), we might ask: is painting to sculpture as male (culture) is to female (nature)?[8]

Thirteen years after his 1846 *Salon*, Baudelaire's dismissal of sculpture is replaced by a keen morbid fascination with the art. Although painting continues to occupy the throne in the Baudelairian palace of the arts, the critic is no longer bored before the sculptural. By 1859, he has discovered an attractive intimacy between sculpture and death and he now argues for the sculptural representation of a certain neglected object, "It is generally held . . . that the skeleton should be excluded from the realm of sculpture. This is a great error" (*Art in Paris* 211). Baudelaire's association of sculpture and death is not neutral with regard to sexual difference – his examples of skeletal statues are female. Two works by Ernest Christophe are Baudelaire's particular favorites and the subject of his essay's exuberant last few pages. One of these works may be observed from two points of view; frontally it represents a smiling woman, but from an angle her expression is one of agony. This time the possibility of multiple points of view does not tire Baudelaire. The laughing woman is an actress who masks a tragic reality and is the inspiration for the poet's "Le Masque." Baudelaire begins his description of Christophe's second statue, which represents a decomposed beauty, in this way: "Imagine a great female skeleton all ready to set out for a revel" (213). Quoting from his "Danse macabre," the critic then evokes the grotesque feminine, "Her deep eyes are wells of darkness and shadow, and her skull, tastefully

---

[8] In terms of Ortner's classic essay, "Is Female to Male as Nature is to Culture?" it should be clarified that sculpture is indeed a product of culture, but an ambiguous product that reasserts the proximity of woman and nature. The sculptural artifacts of the Caribs discussed by Baudelaire are cultural products, but they fail to achieve what he would term the transcendental character of painting.

crowned with flowers, sways slackly on her slender spine. – Oh spell of nothingness, madly bedecked!" (214 n1). (The poet's subject performs the same dance as the now deceased Evelyn Habal, whom Edison compares to "nothingness" [110, 888].) Baudelaire's appreciation of sculpture thus involves a correspondence between the stone image, the skeleton (death), the artificial, and the feminine, the same correspondence that runs through *L'Eve future*.

A syntagmatic association between sculpture, death, and the feminine surely accounts in part for the discomfort that has led many to both fetishize and "iconoclastize" this form of representation. The anxiety surrounding the notion of sculpture is apparently overdetermined; numerous properties of the stone image may promote ambivalence, including sculpture's principal subject, the human body, its reliance on the material (stone, earth), its mechanical or industrial character,[9] and fear or even doubt concerning the statue's immobility (*sculpture* derives from *static*, after all), a fear that may be at the root of the Pygmalion myth. Each of these qualities of sculpture in turn implicates the feminine. Furthermore, Baudelaire's reproach that sculpture denies the spectator a unique point of view may be related to a fundamental fear of the object in three-dimensions, a "metaphysical fear of space" (Read 38).

A close association between death and the object is the subject of Serres's *Statues*, a study that seeks to establish a philosophy of the object, "We seek to describe the emergence of the object, not only of the tool or the beautiful statue but of the thing in general, ontologically speaking. How did the object arise in humanity?" (162).[10] The statue is a privileged object in this ontology because it exposes the primal relationship between subject and object, cleaved by death. Death is the catalyst that transforms the living body (subject) into a work of art (object) (144). The corpse and by extension the mummy are humanity's original objects/statues:

> The cadaver was the first object for men . . . The first solid also . . . the first stone statue . . .

---

[9] Burnham's work is an essential study of sculpture's status as technical object in the twentieth century. Sculptures have long been associated with the mechanical, however, from Daedalus's moving statues to the automaton musicians of the eighteenth century. Many critics have displayed disdain for the physical nature of the sculptural activity. A class distinction has obviously been drawn between the arts of painting and sculpture.

[10] Translations of *Statues* are mine.

> Work on the dead body then objectifies it and solidifies it anew . . . the embalmer separates the solid from the fluid, the firm from the soft, the stable from the unstable, form from chaos, the distinct from the indistinct, the bones from the entrails. Emergence and constitution, I mean by this latter term the stabilization of bodies and the birth of statues. (163)

Serres is describing what Baudelaire and Gautier had illustrated, that the work of art (mummy) is a dressed-up corpse (skeleton). Yet, as the two nineteenth-century writers make clear, the mummy is more often than not fantasized as a *mommy*, for a female corpse lies beneath the textual wrappings that preserve and contain their works of art.

Villiers recognized this fundamental significance of sculpture and, like Baudelaire and Gautier, projected it onto his female characters. The *andréide* lives in an underground, artificial and utopian space in the company of Algonquin mummies:

> [Edison is speaking] I've discovered under this house of mine, at a depth of several hundred feet, two enormous underground caves, formerly the burial grounds of the aboriginal Algonquin tribes who in ancient ages used to inhabit this area . . . In the second [cave] I have stored, with all reverence, the mummified bodies and powdery bones of our sachems, and then closed up the entrance to this underground cemetery, no doubt forever. (88, 866)

Evelyn Habal's resting place is also in this sepulchral chamber. Moreover, Hadaly, who lives in the first cave, travels as an Egyptian princess sealed in a coffin "[with] an interior of black satin which exactly modeled a feminine form" (204, 998). Her fetishes accompany her:

> One would have thought it a modern improvement on an Egyptian coffin, suitable for the burial of a Cleopatra. To the right and to the left in compartments of the walls were ranged a dozen strips of magnetic tin, like funerary scrolls, a manuscript, a ring of glass, and various other items of equipment. (204, 998)

Metal strips and a manuscript are the wrappings of this technological mummy. Hadaly is, originally and most importantly, a cadaver –

this is suggested in numerous passages, from the dissection scene to the presentation of the custom-made coffin. Edison and Ewald are not mere connoisseurs of sculpture and archaeology, they are necrophiles whose search for the source of the feminine leads them to the statue's birthplace: the mummy's tomb.

My undertaking in this chapter is a modest one. I do not intend to propose a theoretical framework for the study of the representation of women in sculpture; rather, I want to expose several aspects of the nineteenth century's discourse on sculpture and the feminine through an analysis of *L'Eve future*. As Serres suggests, our knowledge of the object is perhaps best advanced through the reading of texts, and *L'Eve future* is an invaluable text for such an endeavor. In it, Villiers constructs a veritable museum of the object in all its manifestations, ancient and modern: the body, the work of art, and the technical object.

[B] GROUNDING SCULPTURE

In his 1821 essay, "A Commentary on an Antique Statue of Venus found on the Island of Milos," Quatremère de Quincy describes Greek creativity as eternally renewable:

> Even if we had a hundred thousand statues, a hundred thousand pieces, come directly or indirectly from their [Greek] schools, one could be discovered tomorrow which would reveal to us, in one way or another, a way of seeing or imitating nature, different from that known before, and superior in its way to the works already possessed. (17-18)

Like Edison and Ewald's mechanical harem, Greek soil yields an infinite number of unique images. Writing at the inception of an age that would mass-duplicate *oeuvres d'art* – transforming them into *objets d'art* – and enclose the originals behind museum walls, Quatremère recognized the urgency of defending the originality of Greek works. His declaration may therefore be interpreted as an apology for the modern acquisition of antique chefs-d'oeuvre. His paradoxical assessment of Greek art as numerous originals recalls Edison's lengthy discourse on artifice, comedy and the absence of sincerity in the modern world, although the inventor's discussion is tongue-in-cheek whereas Quatremère's is (sincerely) serious. For both, however, originality and multiplicity are intricately interwoven.

Quatremère's discourse on the possibility of identifying an original work of art takes the form of a comparison of the (re)productive powers of Egypt, Greece, and Rome. This maternal metaphor reminds the reader that one of the astounding feats of the mother is that she may reproduce numerous distinct offspring from the same material or body. The inability of the male body to mimic this achievement is perhaps responsible for Edison's final decision to produce one prototypic daughter who would lack distinctive sisters but herself contain all women. Edison (actually, Villiers) intricately weaves together nineteenth-century French views of Egyptian, Greek and Roman art in his creation of the ideal feminine as both eternal and modern. Quatremère's fundamental essay delineates these views.

Returning to Quatremère, the reader finds that the traditional Romantic metaphor for artistic genius, fertility, is used to distinguish the three ancient cultures, as the question "Where do babies come from?" is displaced by "Where do works of art come from?" Egypt, the first in this lineage of civilizations, is sterile: "Egypt, in matters of art, was and always will be sterile . . . In actual fact (understood in the moral sense) there is and there has been but a single figure, a single head, a single edifice, a single bas-relief, a single painting in Egypt. All Egypt was condemned to uniformity . . . " (17). With a model of beauty already well-established, Egyptian art can only reproduce the same tired original. Roman soil, on the other hand, has as the genesis of its aesthetic code a derivation. Like Alicia's repertoire of melodies, Roman productions have been and always will be reproductions. Relying on Greek originals, Rome contented itself with (oftentimes bad) copies, and became a marketplace for redundant works of art. Finally, between sterility and compulsive repetition lies the fertility of Greek soil – only the Greek mother can eternally bear heterogeneous masterpieces.

Quatremère identifies early nineteenth-century France with the Roman or final stage of his history of representation (and we might suggest that late nineteenth-century France coincides with Rome's decadent period). France (and Europe in general) is displaying a passion for Greek works similar to that experienced in ancient Rome, "The multiplicity of the antique products has propagated the taste for them throughout all the countries, and this taste has also contributed to making the discoveries more and more numerous in Italy" (16-17). And more and more problematic, Quatremère continues. In fact, the discovery of ancient statues necessitates an entirely new discourse on originality, including new criteria for judging the real value of a work, since beauty no longer sufficiently guarantees a work as original (16-17, 19).[11] In the same way, Alicia's beauty cannot forever cloak her status as forgery. Edison and Sowana are, or wish to be, Greeks in Roman days. The greatest paradox of *L'Eve future* is perhaps just this: from a copy, an original is produced. And this is indeed the newly discovered reproductive power of technology. The conflict between Greece and Rome, between the original and counterfeit, is resolved — modern copies will all be originals.

Early in the nineteenth century, Quatremère fell upon an issue that would in time radically alter the status of the work of art. Beauty, a judgment based on a tradition or code of aesthetics, cannot apply to copies or works that are ahistorical. As the work is politicized or circulated in society, it loses its *authenticity*, to use Benjamin's term ("The presence of the original is the prerequisite to the concept of authenticity" [222]), what Berger calls its *authority* ("What the modern means of reproduction have done is to destroy the authority of art..." [32]). The age of mechanical reproduction, beginning with lithography and culminating in photography and film (and including photosculpture), has destroyed the possibility of an original, which Quatremère presciently proposes to reinstate with his *multiplicity of originals*. Rome, enamored of "degenerate productions" (16), resembles modern France, decadent in its proliferation of art objects. Alicia represents the degenerate goddess of her

---

[11] Despite Quatremère's hesitation to label a work as original, he cannot help but make an exception for the *Venus de Milo*, "... we are not able to pronounce the word 'original' in an absolute sense at the sight of even the most beautiful works ... If, on the other hand, one wishes to use the word in a sense relative to the superiority of different examples of the same work, there cannot be I feel, any reason to doubt that the Venus de Milo, in the group of which it originally was a part, was the original of those we have named" (19-20). The *Venus* is an original by virtue of its relationship to (imaginary) reproductions. It was argued in the late nineteenth century, however, that this statue had been falsely dated as a Classical piece when it was really of the Hellenistic period. For elaboration on this misattribution and its relation to *L'Eve future*, see my "The Decadent Goddess: *L'Eve future* and the *Venus de Milo*." Huet also discusses the Venus statue and *L'Eve future* in her study.

era – her beauty is not indicative of authenticity, authority, and tradition, but of a fragmentary and ultimately negated resemblance to an original. Hadaly, however, although she is a copy, will attain a certain aura – the aura of modernity which Quatremère had begun to sketch.

Quatremère's grounding of sculpture in soil that is either infer-. tile or fertile (ideally or decadently so) is echoed in the Hegelian vegetal metaphor for aesthetic growth and decline:

> Each art has its time of efflorescence, of its perfect development as an art, and a history preceding and following this moment of perfection. For the products of all the arts are works of the spirit and therefore are not, like natural productions, complete all at once within their specific sphere; on the contrary, they have a beginning, a progress, a perfection, and an end, a growth, blossoming, and decay. (Hegel 2: 614)

This image of the stages or seasons of nature belongs to an idealist and Romantic discourse on art history (see Bungay). In *L'Eve future*, Alicia Clary and Evelyn Habal represent a period of decay of the sculptural figure, and a decay of the Romantic ideal. In terms of reproduction, all the women of *L'Eve future* are "sterile": Hadaly is a sexual being, but is not capable of reproduction; Alicia does not plan on reproducing; and Evelyn uses birth control. In this modern period of eternal winter, Hadaly is, however, meant to be a modern sculptural example of fertility and rejuvenation in her stance as a copy without an original.

Far from ideal, Alicia and Evelyn are, in terms of appearance, merely "pleasing" or "agreeable" (Evelyn is not beautiful, but *jolie*), those terms that Hegel uses to characterize contemporary French culture (2: 620). The pleasing style emphasizes the external effects of beauty, that is, beauty's effect on the spectator. Hegel (followed by Baudelaire) identifies this "production of effects" with a proliferation of accessories:

> In architecture, sculpture, and painting, the pleasing style produces the disappearance of simple and grand masses; everywhere we see little independent miniatures, decoration, ornaments, dimples on the cheeks, graceful coiffures, smiles, robes variously draped, attractive colours and forms, poses that are striking and difficult and yet unconstrained and alive. (2: 618-19)

Evelyn and Alicia's performances display no spiritual depth; their sole purpose is to motivate the base passions of male spectators. Evelyn's *danse macabre* is a literal "production of effects" and after her death her *personal effects* are her accessories, collected by Edison and stored in a drawer/coffin that serves as museum or mausoleum. As for Alicia, the bourgeois beauty signals the decay of the Greek ideal. Ideal *Venus* has turned outward, seeking justification in the eyes of those who behold her.

Paradoxically, Hadaly herself is the supreme example of a pleasing work of art, since her existence depends entirely upon Ewald's perception of her. But whereas Evelyn's accessories are negative effects, Hadaly's sculptural ornamentation has undergone, to borrow Schor's phrase, a "sublimation of the detail" (*Reading* 35). Schor categorizes Hegel's *Aesthetics* as a move to transform the accessorial into the chef-d'oeuvre, "It would not be exaggerated to claim that the transformation of the so-called insignificant object into an art-object engages the entire *Aesthetics* . . . " (36). This is precisely Edison and Sowana's move: the metamorphosis of the ornamental into an aura-inspiring ideal, as Alicia and Evelyn, faulty *objets d'art*, are transformed into the *chef-d'oeuvre* called Hadaly.

This aspect of Hadaly's contradictory nature brings us back to Edison's discourse on sincerity. In "Nothing New under the Sun" Edison follows the contradiction to its logical end: if the android is to represent all women, she must herself be insincere. But whereas Alicia is insincerely insincere, Hadaly will be sincerely insincere. She is an actress, but a good one, just as she is a good copy of the *Venus de Milo*. Hadaly takes her comedy roles seriously, "[Edison is speaking] she's a marvelous actress, endowed, if you'll take my word, with a talent far more concentrated, more sure of itself, and certainly much more *serious* than that of Miss Alicia Clary" (84-85, 862). Alicia, relying on illusion, can only copy *poorly*, that is, repeat acts that were originally mere reproductions. Like the hypnotized hysteric, the virtuosa performs in a *mise en abîme* of artifice whereas Hadaly is cast (literally) in multiple molds or roles, each as unique as the next.

L'Eve future thus reveals a nineteenth-century obsession with the proliferation of cloned *objets d'art*. Whether we call this process a "bibelotization" (Saisselin) or "reification" (Williams) of the (art) object, the result is a hallucinated animation of the object, accompanied by passivity on the part of the subject (as in several of Gautier's works). Edison, suffering perhaps from "statuomania," originally intends to construct a series of *andréides* with Hadaly as the first of these assembly-line automata. As a truly modern work of art, she must be reproduced.[12] Hadaly is *designed* for mass-production. Edison, who possesses her "formula" (217, 1013), means to cure mankind of its ills with the aid of "thousands and thousands of . . . facsimiles" (164, 951). Alicia's aberrant resemblance to the *Venus de Milo* justifies the scientist's project, "what is strange is that this sublime monstrosity arrived in the world just in time to provide a proof of my first Android" (181, 969). The bad copy necessitates an endless production of bibelots and one day the fabrication of androids will constitute an entire industry:

> Only the first Android was difficult. Once the general formula was written, as I've said before, all that remained was a kind of handicraft work. There's no doubt that within a few years substrata like this one will be fabricated by the thousands; the first manufacturer who picks up the idea will be able to establish a factory for the production of Ideals! (147, 930)

Industry has democratized the ideal feminine and is intent on its efficient and economical reproduction. As Gautier points out in respect to photosculpture, pure art seems expensive to a thrifty century.

In fact however, only Edison's renunciation of his female factory at the end of the novel ("I shall make no more androids" [217, 1013]) allows Hadaly to take her place as an *original* work of art – a chef-d'oeuvre who "jams" all codes like a computer virus antidote that would halt an endless and thus meaningless reproduction of (mis)information. Hadaly escapes the infinite series of works by terminating the aesthetic code, as does *Sarrasine*'s masterpiece:

> The Zambinellan body is a real body; but this real body is total (glorious, miraculous) only insofar as it descends from a body already written by statuary (Ancient Greece, Pygmalion); it too (like the other bodies in *Sarrasine*) is a replica, issuing from a code. This code is infinite since it is written. Yet the duplicative

---

[12] On statuomania, see Agulhon's article. On reproduction as a requirement of the modern work of art, see Benjamin, "the work of art reproduced becomes the work of art designed for reproducibility" (226).

chain may assert its origin and the Code declare itself grounded, stopped, jammed. This grounding, this stoppage, this jamming of the Code, is the *masterpiece*. (S/Z 114-15)

Hadaly interrupts and arrests a possibly infinite series of photo-sculpted Eves. Because Hadaly must be an original, Alicia will pose not as the *Venus* but as Eve (177, 964). Moreover, Edison's renunciation is due in part to Hadaly's refusal to submit to an existence as mere copy; she would instead assume the aura of an authentic work of art. Benjamin's definition of aura, "[the] unique phenomenon of a distance, however close it may be" (224), implies the distance and unapproachability that the android achieves through the possession of a supernatural soul. Edison, unable to fully *comprehend* his creation, realizes the impossibility of *reproducing* her.

As *L'Eve future* makes clear, many privileged objects of mass-production in the nineteenth century are marked as feminine. Benjamin does not characterize the age of mechanical reproduction in terms of sexual difference, but John Berger's study promotes a distinction between the male and female gaze that in turn gives rise to a gendering of the object. The history of representation, and especially the category of the nude, has been, Berger argues, governed by this distinction:

> One might simplify [this] by saying: *men act* and *women appear*. Men look at women. Women watch themselves being looked at. This determines not only most relations between men and women but also the relation of women to themselves. The surveyor of woman in herself is male: the surveyed female. Thus she turns herself into an object – and most particularly an object of vision: a sight. (47)

This assessment of the female psyche echoes Freud's estimation of women as narcissistic and bisexual; the male within woman renders her, through his gaze, a work of art – a canvas, a sculpture, a photograph. Woman sees herself as *represented*, not as *representing*. She is always already a copy, miming and imitating to please her private male spectator. She is not permitted to create, but only to generate bad copies in a Roman house of mirrors that denies her a stable and unique identity, the latter attained only when man has represented her. According to this logic, technological reproduction is a feminine form of representation that produces bad copies to be faxed and photocopied in an endless proliferation that, on rare occasions, culminates in a mechanical masterpiece, a Hadaly.

If bibelotization is an essentially femininizing process, then the sculpted *objet d'art* is a feminine object. The bibelot ("a small house-hold ornament or decorative object" [*Websters*]) found one of its primary incarnations in the nineteenth century as the *Venus de Milo*. Furthermore, women maintain an intimate but ambiguous relationship to the bibelot; they are both consumed by and consumers of this incessant flow of knickknacks, just as Evelyn Habal collects her accoutrements and artificial limbs, "Women became the rival of the work of art. She turned into a bibelot herself, surrounded by bibelots, an expensive object of desire, to be possessed and cherished, but also exhibited" (Saisselin 62). The demimondaine, that obscure and obscured object of desire, is the star exhibitionist in this open market of art objects; she is an actress whose theater is any and every public space (Saisselin 55). Once again, the female performer most succinctly characterizes her era. In *L'Eve future*, the aristocratic collector, Ewald, disillusioned by the bourgeois bibelot, seeks and finds in Hadaly a true masterpiece or that which refuses to be bibelotized. However, Hadaly's unwillingness to circulate foreshadows her death, for true masterpieces must be buried (as was the *Venus de Milo* for so many centuries) in the museum/cemetery. The feminine that refuses to reproduce – that refuses to serve as a model for endless reproduction – is the monstrous feminine, and is banned from the modern artist's studio.

This same phenomenon of the mass-production and circulation of *objets d'art* regulates the relationship between the photographic image and the feminine. Photography is, like sculpture, an art that promotes animation and thus enables the female characters of *L'Eve future* to circulate as living representations. The photographic *carte de visite* replaces the sculptural *Venus de Milo* as the symbol of this metamorphosis. Hypnosis, a favored theme of nineteenth-century narratives, is also intimately associated with metamorphosis and – although this association has not often been cited – the sculptural. Hypnosis is both a symptom and cure of what ails the feminine in the nineteenth century. Three nineteenth-century scientists, one of them in his fictional form, used this association to their benefit in their work: Villiers's Thomas Edison, J.-M. Charcot, and Sigmund Freud.

[C] The Hypnotic Feminine[13]

In October of 1885, Sigmund Freud – then a young dozent in neuropathology at the University of Vienna – arrived in Paris on a travelling bursary to study under Jean-Martin Charcot, Chair of Neurology at the Salpêtrière Hospital. Although he expected to pursue his neurological studies at the clinic, Charcot's dynamic personality and original insights into hysteria determined Freud to turn his attention to the psychological. Charcot's legacy to psychoanalysis included his research on hypnosis, a phenomenon with which Freud was already familiar upon his arrival at the Salpêtrière. A derivative of mesmerism – itself a brand of animal magnetism – hypnosis was named in 1840 by the Scottish doctor James Braid. Leaving behind the mesmerist's paraphernalia (*baquets*, magnets and wands), the hypnotist gained access through suggestion to a passive subject's "private theater," to use Anna O.'s term. Charcot's privileged technique in the demonstration of hysteria, hypnosis was later renounced by Freud in favor of free association. Yet the specter of suggestion haunted Freud long after the "âge d'or"[14] of hypnosis, as evinced in his comparison of the transference to suggestion, "It must dawn on us that in our technique we have abandoned hypnosis only to rediscover suggestion in the form of the transference" (16: 446).[15]

In March 1886, as Freud's studies in Paris came to an end, the journal *La Vie Moderne* concluded its publication in serial form of *L'Eve future*, which appeared in book form in May 1886. Villiers's novel is in part a fantastic transcription of and musing on the inves-

---

[13] A version of this section has appeared in *The Romanic Review* with the title "*L'Eve future* and the Hypnotic Feminine."

[14] Barrucand uses this term to refer to the period 1880-90. I use the terms hypnosis and suggestion interchangeably in this section, although in the latter nineteenth century a clear distinction was drawn between them. The Nancy School, under H. Bernheim, insisted that hypnosis was nothing but psychological suggestion and that all were susceptible to it. Charcot defined hypnosis more narrowly as a psychosomatic symptom of hysteria. Freud oscillated between the two views while maintaining a filial loyalty to Charcot.

[15] Indeed, a new golden age of hypnosis has recently dawned in theories that, in placing emphasis on Freud's comments on suggestion, posit a fundamental hypnotic or passive phase preceding the birth of the Freudian subject (Borch-Jacobsen, Roustang).

tigations concerning hypnosis that occupied both medical circles and the general public at the time. Villiers doubtless heard talk of Charcot from his literary peers: Maupassant attended Charcot's lessons, as did Léon Daudet. 1886 thus saw both a monumental moment in the history of psychoanalysis – its incorporation of hypnosis [16] – and a finalized version of the work that had occupied Villiers since the late 1870s. Indeed, a notable modification in the definitive version of the text is its added emphasis on hypnosis; whereas *L'Eve nouvelle* of 1880-81 does not present suggestion as a tool for the fabrication of the ideal female android, its successor in 1885-86 includes numerous references to magnetism and hypnosis.

L'Eve future's hypnotic scenes depend on a link between suggestion and the art of sculpture, and this association is historically linked to Freud's work on hysterical paralysis, a condition demonstrated repeatedly by Charcot at the Salpêtrière. More precisely, the nineteenth century's fascination with hypnosis and the early adoption of the technique by psychoanalysis are concomitant with a mania for classical sculptural representations of women, in particular the *Venus de Milo*. Hypnotic stances and sculptural relics thus converge in a will to fragment that characterizes medical discourse on female anatomy. This fragmentation, accompanied by the paralytic immobility of the hypnotic trance, deprives woman of anatomical self-awareness, reducing her to a formless stone block awaiting the inscriptions of the hypnotist and chiseler. As with technological reproductions of the artwork, the production of woman as hypnotic subject denies the existence of an original model: individual women no longer exist and "woman" is created by the scientist and artist.

An example from Charcot's numerous lectures on hypnosis illustrates the relationship of hypnosis to the sculpted remains that preoccupy Lord Ewald. Charcot, regarded as the first to consider hysteria a veritable disease, regularly displayed a succession of (predominantly) female hysterics to a (predominantly) male audience during his Tuesday Lessons, posing the women in various positions by means of induced or artificial hypnosis. A typical example of

---

[16] Of course, this moment is more difficult to pinpoint than implied here. Joseph Breuer had been employing hypnosis as a therapeutic method for several years (the case of Anna O. dates from 1882). Freud introduced hypnosis in his practice in the form of direct suggestion late in 1887, and Breuer's cathartic method in 1889.

Charcot's procedure is the lesson of January 24, 1888, which describes the following stimulation of arm paralysis:

> The slap was given with the palm of the hand, and the arm and shoulder were brought into play. One can make almost no use of the shoulder with a slap of the back of the hand – only the elbow is affected – while with a slap of the palm, the shoulder and the entire arm are affected; consequently one should see in this instance an arm paralysis, and this is what has occurred.
> First the latter slap was effected, then the former.
> This is a complete paralysis of the arm; consequently, the amputation line must include the entire shoulder. (104)[17]

This description compulsively repeats the four terms that define the (female) forelimb: hand, arm, elbow, and shoulder. Charcot distinguishes degrees of arm paralysis – two slaps suffice to freeze the entire limb for analysis. What is perhaps most striking in this lesson, and I shall return to this crucial point, is Charcot's subsequent assertion that his mastery has robbed the hysteric of self-knowledge, that is, of corporeal awareness. As the doctor notes, "This woman has no idea where her arm is" (105). She will become anatomically conscious only after Charcot has "returned" her arm.

This disassembling and reassembling of the female body is fictionalized in *L'Eve future*'s "hypnotic" scenes, prime examples of the literary representation of nineteenth-century sculptural and medical positioning or imaging of woman. Hypnosis and its related disorder, somnambulism, afflict nearly all of the novel's characters and particularly the women. In creating such sleepy women, Villiers follows a tradition exemplified by E.T.A. Hoffmann. What distinguishes Villiers's enterprise is his lengthy metaphysician's treatment of the relationship of hypnosis to the very being of woman. Edison's fabrication of woman is not presented, as it is in Georges du Maurier's *Trilby* for example, as the dastardly deed of a maniac who abuses hypnosis (although this cliché is hinted at in *L'Eve future*), but as an intensely serious attempt to define and revise the essence of femininity. Sowana is under hypnosis throughout the novel, Edison himself works while in a somnambulant trance, and Hadaly will be

---

[17] Page references are to *L'Hystérie*, a selection of Charcot's essays edited by E. Trillat. Translations are mine. The *Leçons du mardi* include drawings that clearly demarcate amputation lines on the patient's body.

a somnambulist once she arrives in England. In addition, Evelyn Habal is hypnotized before she is captured on film by the scientist. Finally, Alicia Clary is portrayed as the most susceptible to hypnosis. In one scene for example, Sowana literally petrifies Alicia, turning her to stone to copy her form for transference to Hadaly. That Alicia is easily hypnotized comes as no surprise given her profession: she is a performer who mimes the roles dictated to her by male mentors, her Svengalis.

Edison's "petrification" of Alicia is one instance of a preoccupation in *L'Eve future* with the artificial arm – the floating signifier that Chambers has labeled the essential symbol of the novel ("L'Ange" 47). By virtue of this insistence on the representational power of the arm, the novel becomes an account of the restitution of the *Venus de Milo*'s lost arms. Since Alicia is a disappointing copy of the *Venus*, Edison's goal becomes the completion and perfection of the ancient statue through the addition of artificial arms, those of the android, paving the way for its resurrection in the nineteenth century. Not surprisingly, the female arms are a deciding factor in the degree of resemblance between Alicia and the *Venus*. The performer herself points out the anatomical discrepancy between her body and the carved one during a visit to the Louvre. Lord Ewald has taken Alicia to see the statue purposely, hoping the likeness will inspire a hint of spirituality in the positivist – but no such luck. "Look, it's *me*!" Alicia cries, but then immediately adds, "Yes, but **I** have arms, and besides I'm more distinguished looking" (46, 816). Alicia's dismal assessment of her resemblance to the statue, that is, her lack of knowledge of her own body, is precisely what has led Ewald to suicidal thoughts.

The female arm, appearing throughout the text, establishes the undercurrent of disintegration and restoration of the feminine that pervades and sustains *L'Eve future*. For example, Edison's monologue, with which the text opens, quickly mutates into a dialogue between the male protagonist and an absent woman represented by her arm, lying amputated on a cushion (this woman truly does not know where her arm is). In this way, the true central character of the novel, the artificial feminine, is introduced:

> By accident, the paper [Ewald's telegram] dropped on an object of a striking and remarkable character – an object whose very presence in such a place was inexplicable. Accidental as it

was, the juncture of these two objects seemed to attract Edison's attention; he paused, considering the event and reflecting on it . . .

It was a human arm, lying on a cushion of violet silk. (17, 780)

The hypnotic limb signifies the inventor's past destruction of female life, for it has supposedly been severed in a train accident that occurred in the course of an experiment. (The limb is a very literal embodiment of "railway spine," a term that referred to paralyses resulting from traumatic events such as train accidents; Charcot devoted a lecture to the subject.) It also signifies Edison's present venture, the construction of Hadaly, who is generated from the principles that this arm – in reality artificial – represents. The scientist then turns out the lights, but the artifact will not be obscured, "The pale light caressed that inanimate hand, wandered across the arm, lit up the eyes of the golden viper, and caused the blue ring to sparkle" (19, 782). This passage will be echoed in the final paragraph of the novel when, after reading Ewald's second (farewell) telegram, Edison is drawn to the magnetic arm, "a beam of moonlight fell whitely on that charming arm, on the pale hand with its enchanted rings" (219, 1017). Edison cannot seem to rid himself of this grisly knickknack, the appendage with which the text opens and closes and that gives rise, philosophically and scientifically, to the android who constitutes the body of the text.

The reproduction compulsion that drives the fictional Edison also determines Charcot's use of suggestion. According to the latter, paralyses of the hand can be artificially reproduced under certain circumstances (that is, under hypnosis), a phenomenon that constitutes "the sublime in this matter and the ideal as regards pathological physiology" (*L'Hystérie* 99). The dialectic of the artificial and the real, the copy and the original, on which the premise of *L'Eve future* rests characterizes the dynamics of suggestion and often centers, as in the novel, on the arm. Artificial hypnosis – that induced by the doctor – is countered and mimicked by auto-hypnosis, a state brought on by the patient herself. In fact, real or natural hypnosis is no less a representation, for it is the symptom of an *unnatural* condition called hysteria, "Naturally, we seek to reproduce hysterical paralyses, it is not in our power to reproduce organic states" (101). Exact reproduction of a *copy* is Charcot's method of inquiry, and Edison follows Charcot in his choice of Alicia, a *Venus de Milo* look-alike, as model for Hadaly.

In yet another passage that evokes the female arm as a symbol of feminine artifice, Alicia's limbs are frozen into stone and her eyelids shut, thus transforming her momentarily into a modern and restored *Venus de Milo*. In the chapter entitled "Suggestion," Edison hypnotizes Alicia in order to speak privately with Lord Ewald. He does so not with a slap, but with a wave of his magnetic palm:

> Softly, gradually, her lids closed over her lustrous eyes; her arms, as if petrified into Paros marble, remained motionless, one resting on the table, the other, still holding its bouquet of pale roses, resting on a cushion.
>
> Like a statue of the Olympian Venus rigged out in modern dress, she seemed fixed in this attitude; and the beauty of her features, in this posture, seemed almost superhuman.
>
> Lord Ewald, who had seen the hypnotic gestures and the effect of instant torpor, took Alicia's hand, now suddenly cold. (178, 965-66)

In this scene, *Venus Alicia* has no idea where her arm is, an arm that doubles the artificial limb contemplated earlier by Edison and that also rested on a cushion. Alicia's limbs are then doubled and displaced by those of the artificial Hadaly, who has entered the room, "remaining silent, motionless, and attentive behind her dark veil, her silver arms crossed over her breast" (179, 966). All female arms in *L'Eve future* (and this includes Evelyn Habal's) are, in the final analysis, simulacra subject to exchange.

The contrast between Alicia and the *Venus de Milo* mirrors the discrepancy between the real woman's mediocre character and ideal form. Ewald recollects that "between the body and the soul of Miss Alicia, it wasn't just a disproportion which distressed and upset my understanding; it was an absolute *disparity*" (31, 798). After meeting Alicia, Edison – doctor and psychotherapist as well as inventor – diagnoses this disparity as a pathological deformity, "Her resemblance to the *Venus Victorious* is nothing for her but a kind of elephantiasis of which she will die. A pathological deformity with which her wretched little nature is afflicted" (181, 969). Edison's choice of the word *elephantiasis* is telling: this disease would yield an unnaturally enlarged limb. Alicia's arm is *de trop*, and its overabundance has negated its value as image. The performer's fault, her original sin, is that she is a *bad* copy of the statue – she cannot properly take the *Venus de Milo*'s place, she can only falsify or forge it, that is, mimic it. Her occupation as a virtuosa, an art that Ewald condemns as pernicious imitation, underscores her inability to produce beautiful reproductions. As Irigaray has noted, this sort of bad imitation is the only recourse left to women in Freud's economy of representation. Incapable of sublimation, woman "simulates" representation:

> Women's special form of neurosis would be to "mimic" a work of art, to be *a bad (copy of a) work of art*. Her neurosis would be recognized as a counterfeit or parody of an artistic process. It is transformed into an aesthetic object, but one without value, which has to be condemned because it is *a forgery*. It is neither "nature" nor an appropriate technique for re-producing nature. (*Speculum* 125)

Villiers also limits real women to the role of bad imitator, using hypnosis as one means of reinforcing and displaying their hysterical physical deformities. From Alicia's diseased limb, a malingering bad copy, the scientist verbally deconstructs real woman, constructing in her place a hypnotic Venus whose arms are neither absent nor *de trop*, but in harmony with her other limbs.

Hypnosis is not only a tool for acquiring the distance and time necessary to re-theorize the feminine, however. Edison recalls Breuer and Freud in his further application of the technique as a means to a cure, two cures to be precise. He provides Ewald with a mesmerizing mate, Hadaly, fulfilling Freud's insights concerning the association between love, hypnosis, and transference ("From being in love to hypnosis is evidently only a short step" [18: 114]), and he employs hypnosis in an attempt to recover Sowana's "true" self. But the somnambulist, like Freud's infamous Dora, escapes her master's will before the transference or hypnotic bond is entirely (dis)solved. Indeed, Sowana's transference into Hadaly's body attests to her ability to simulate hypnosis and use it to her own ends.

Any Sowana's former self, the reader learns well into the novel, is a certain Mistress Anderson, the wife of Edison's friend who committed suicide after squandering his happy home and finances on Evelyn Habal (this suicide both prompts Edison's desire to prevent another and foreshadows it). The scientist explains to Ewald that when Mistress Anderson developed a sleeping sickness after Anderson's death, Edison intervened, separated the mother from her children, and commenced a cure by establishing the flow of his magnetic fluid (or will) into his patient with a set of iron rings and telephone lines. Whereas Alicia's brand of hysteria – that of the incurable performer – has prompted Edison to use suggestion primarily as a *demonstrative tool* (as did Charcot), Sowana is the subject of a *therapeutic cure* that identifies the patient (*à la Freud*) as suffering from reminiscences. Edison's project fails, however, not because Mistress Anderson's affections have been transferred onto the hypnotist – as happened with Anna O. and Breuer – but because her spirit, called Sowana, has willingly transferred itself into the android. Unlike Edison, Ewald recognizes Sowana's escape from her analyst. Concerning her "cure," he says to Edison, "Cure her? . . . Transfigure her, rather" (209, 1003). Edison has in one sense cured his patient, for she has been relieved of the traumatic remembrance of her past and restored to a primal self, but this cure has been effected *in spite of* the hypnotist's efforts. As the scientist and supposed locus of knowledge says himself, "though I know Mrs. Anderson, *I swear to you on my soul* THAT I DO NOT KNOW SOWANA!" (211, 1007). Mistress Anderson has, it would appear, cured herself through a self-induced trance that causes her somnambulism. She may then remove herself from Edison's apparatus of wires and rings and merge with Hadaly, a transmutation that the scientist interprets – perhaps too hastily – as her death.

Sowana's powers are not limited to self-metamorphosis. As Auerbach shows, the nineteenth-century transformed woman is also a transforming figure.[18] Sowana's susceptibility to hypnosis is highlighted by a skill at inducing somnambulant states in others, as Edison says, "'The state of constant spirituality and supreme visionary insight at which *the real life* of Sowana unfolds, confers on her intense powers of suggestion, especially with subjects already half-hypnotized by me" (214, 1010-11). Ewald tells Edison that Sowana has hypnotized Alicia, freezing her in order to draft her form, "this strange sculptress massaged her [*l'a 'comme pétrie'*] for a full half-hour, from head to foot" (208, 1002). This scene echoes Edison's hypnosis of that other female performer, Evelyn Habal. It also points to a further association between the sculptural act and hypnosis: in a reversal of the Pygmalion myth, the real woman becomes

---

[18] See Auerbach and Tatar for discussions of other fictional accounts of the hypnotic bond. Bellour briefly discusses hypnosis in *L'Eve future* in his article.

stone, a *Venus* that will serve as artificial copy and model in the creation of the futuristic Galatea.

Some of the insights gained by Freud during his stay in Paris were published in 1893 in the original French version of "Organic and Hysterical Paralyses," a study that recalls Charcot's interest in the inhibition of movement in hypnotized hysterics while it stakes out new territory. Freud's remarks on paralysis, which was closely related to hypnosis in Charcot's work, shed light on Hadaly's peculiar stance as a hysterical apparition formed of paralyzed female body parts. This article is a textual symptom of what Charles Bernheimer has recently called – in reference to this article and to Freud's theory of sublimation – the "traumatized relation to the 'natural' female body" of fin-de-siècle writers (261n49).[19] In it, Freud first distinguishes between two types of organic paralyses. *Periphero-spinal paralysis* is an organic disorder that affects individual muscle fibers; it is "détaillé." Also called "projection paralysis," this lesion operates by correspondence: an equal number of fibers are affected in the journey from the periphery to the cord. It should be added that this type of paralysis occurs randomly, as "there is no fixed rule according to which one peripheral element escapes paralysis while another suffers from it permanently" (1: 161). No one element or part of the body is privileged by the projection disorder. *Cerebral paralysis* is, on the other hand, a paralysis "en masse" – it affects large areas of the body, such as limbs and portions of the extremities. An insufficient number of cord fibers impedes the direct relation of conductive elements to the cortex, and thus the lesion cannot be projected proportionately onto the cortex; it is, rather, a "representation paralysis" that operates by relation.

Concentrating on cerebral paralysis, Freud distinguishes between organic and hysterical afflictions. Whereas periphero-spinal paralysis is always organic, the cerebral type may be simulated by the hysteric, "hysterical paralyses only share the characteristics of organic representation paralyses" (1: 162). And whereas organic cerebral paralysis affects the limbs "en masse," the hysterical version – that presented in the lecture hall by Charcot and represented by Alicia's "elephantiasis" – may result in the isolation, distortion,

---

[19] Bernheimer also notes, "Hysteria ignorant of anatomy: this is precisely the negation of the (female) organic ground so ardently desired by the writers and artists of the decadence and fin de siècle" (261n49).

and dissociation of particular limbs, inasmuch as hysteria is for both Charcot and Freud a disease of "excessive manifestations."

Freud then goes on to declare bluntly that the hysteric's "special sort of representation" robs her of self-knowledge; her manifestations are excessive precisely because they no longer correspond to the category "limb." Hysterical lesions are "completely independent of the anatomy of the nervous system since *in its paralyses and other manifestations hysteria behaves as though anatomy did not exist or as though it had no knowledge of it*" (1: 169). The word *completely* distinguishes Freud's theory from that of Charcot, who continued to search for a "dynamic" lesion at the root of hysterical paralysis. For Freud, hysteria is indeed ignorant of science. Whereas the doctor views limbs as extensions of a whole joined by nerve fibers, the hysteric interprets these limbs "in the ordinary, popular sense of the names they bear: the leg is a leg as far up as its insertion into the hip, the arm is the upper limb as it is visible under the clothing" (1: 169). The hysteric fragments her body, assigning it amputation lines according to perceived notions of anatomy.

As hysteria is linked to the conversion of ideas, so simulated cerebral paralysis involves an "alteration of the *conception*, the *idea*" (1: 170) of the limb in question (Freud's example is the arm). The trauma (such as a railway accident) or lingering "surplus" of affect that has induced hysteria centers associatively on the arm, for instance, and therefore confines the limb to this sole representation, banishing it from the circuit of free association. The arm is no longer available for conscious associative play, the play of ideas that constructs the subject and normally includes the body. Not only is the arm no longer a participant in this game, it insists on its non-existence – it is no longer *there*. The sole idea it is capable of representing is, it would appear, that of *absence*. Autosuggestion and hypnosis, which normally hinder associative powers, may, Freud notes, return the limb to the associative ball park, just as Charcot eventually returns his patient's arm to her. Hypnosis cuts both ways: it cures the illness *and* allows for the artificial return of the disorder's symptoms. In the same way, Edison would cure the ills of his time by replacing living women with simulacra who will, paradoxically, be faultless imitations of their models.

This analysis leads to the ineluctable conclusion that Alicia Clary is the sole stable or non-hysterical female character of *L'Eve future*, for it is Alicia who recognizes and insists before the Venus statue that she indeed possesses arms – "Yes, but **I** have arms." Unlike the other women of Menlo Park, Alicia is *not* ignorant of anatomy. Lacking the knowledge of her *resemblance* to the chef-d'oeuvre, that is, lacking an understanding of her role as image, she asserts her bodily integrity and refuses to participate in Ewald's fantasy of animated artworks. Ewald, threatened by her assertion, can only view Alicia's negation of the resemblance as a sign of ignorance. "If only she would *truly* ignore herself," he most likely sighs, "I could pose her at my will and thus maintain the frozen image of beauty necessary to my very survival." The price paid for beauty in *L'Eve future* is subjection to a process – the archaeological unearthing of sculpture or the hypnotic method – which results in the loss and subsequent wandering of body parts. When faced with the dangers of beauty, one may very well be satisfied to be, like Evelyn Habal, merely *jolie*.

The bulk of *L'Eve future* is devoted to the verbal construction of Hadaly; Edison's narration of the fabrication of a new Eve occupies three times the textual space of her actual participation in the novel's plot. This emphasis on specifically verbal restitution is also valorized in Quatremère's essay on the *Venus de Milo*. On the subject of the possible restoration of the *Venus*'s arms, Quatremère says, "When I speak of it being whole again, I wish to do so verbally; for I believe that not only should it be left in the mutilated state in which it was found, but also that it would be impossible to restore it" (19). This is, finally, the knowledge gained by Edison. Whereas his verbal dissection of the female body is successful – he convinces Ewald of female monstrosity – his attempt to construct an ideal from the mutilated female bodies he amasses is doomed to failure, due perhaps to an ignorance of female anatomy.

The *Venus de Milo* is a favored aesthetic representation of hysterical paralysis in the nineteenth century, as *L'Eve future*'s related discourses on sculpture and hypnosis reveal. The feminine ideal of classical beauty has relegated her arms to non-existence in an acting out of the late nineteenth-century trauma of representation of female sexuality, whose literary symptoms include Freud's article on representation paralysis and Villiers's fetishistic fantasy. Nineteenth-century patriarchy is, these texts suggest, paralyzed or hypnotized before the threat of the female body. Villiers's response to this threat, his mode of disarmament, is typical of a literature obsessed with stone images of women: the male protagonist would appropriate Medusa's power to petrify, that is to fragment sculpturally and hypnotically and thus neutralize the (female) corpus. Typical, but with a (technical) difference, for the story of Hadaly foreshadows twentieth-century literary and cinematic representations of the post-Freudian female monstrosities imagined by science.

CHAPTER 4

PHOTOGRAPHY

Villiers was born in 1838, the year preceding the official invention of photography; his youth corresponds, therefore, to that of the photograph and he belongs to the first generation of writers to be confronted with the new medium for producing images. In fact, *L'Eve future* is one of the earliest, if not *the* earliest French text to present photography as the technique of choice of the modern animator of woman. Villiers thus introduces photography into the narrative history of the aesthetic representation of the ideal female form. In particular, Villiers wrote during the early years of heated controversy surrounding the status of photography, when critics and artists either disputed or upheld photography's membership in the fine arts. Discussions of the aesthetic categories of the real and ideal invariably included references to photography, whose supposed affinity to a real was viewed as either monstrous or liberating. It therefore comes as no surprise that *L'Eve future*'s ideal woman should owe her reality at least in part to the photographic image.

The first half of book 1 records Edison's monologue decrying the late arrival of the phonograph in history. He compares this delayed arrival to that of photography, a technology which like the phonograph was viewed in the nineteenth century as a faithful reproducer of the natural world. In this passage the camera is subordinated to the phonograph, for it is the latter technology that truly defines the historical Edison: he is "the man who made a prisoner of the echo" (7, 767), "the magician of the ear" (7, 768), "a Beethoven of Science" (7, 768) and, of course, "phonograph's papa" (8, 769). This monologue paves the way for *L'Eve future*'s discourse on the human – in particular female – voice. Yet the reader may easily imagine a shift in the emphasis of Edison's speech from the recording of sound to the recording of images, for, as this chapter will argue, photography is more crucial to Edison and Sowana's creation of the feminine than the voice-box.[1]

During his monologue, Edison laments the lack of photographs of world history, "Too bad. For it would have been delightful to possess good photographic prints (taken on the spot) of *Joshua Bidding the Sun Stand Still*, for example. Or why not several different views of *The Earthly Paradise*, taken from the *Gateway of the Flaming Swords*, the *Tree of Knowledge*, the *Serpent*, and so forth?" (22, 786). (Like Joshua, the inventor will bid the sun stand still as he directs a photographic session with Alicia as model.) Sifting through these imaginary photos, Edison – obsessed with the power of reproduction and repetition to dispel doubt – recalls a mythical original Eden on the eve of his revision of the Genesis story, which now includes a photogenic android Eve as centerfold. He is caught throughout most of the novel on the threshold dividing two Edens, a past paradise that is known only from written texts – and not from behind the objective eye of the camera – and a future Eden of his own making. Hesitating in this limbo of incertitude, the otherwise positivist Edison mourns a paradise lost, that paradise whose sounds and images have not been recorded. He dreams, of course, of a paradise found, refound, and found again. His mechanical Eves, cloned with the aide of photography from their beautiful but soulless flesh and blood models, are designed to dispel forever man's doubts regarding the disparity – as Ewald calls it – between the female form and content.

Yes, photography has arrived late in history, Edison sighs. How different the world would appear if we possessed snapshots of crucial events, "photographies de l'histoire du monde" (the Garden of Eden, the Great Flood), mythical figures (Medusa's head, the Furies, Prometheus), famous leaders (Washington, Napoleon, Mohammed) and periods of natural history (the age of the dinosaurs). Edison does not overlook women as subjects for the eye of the apparatus; he would collect images of the illustrious (Joan of Arc, Zenobia) and the beautiful (Venus, Cleopatra, Helen) (22-23, 786-88). Finally, the most appropriate object of photography (and of the

---

[1] For a recent reading of the importance of the voice in *L'Eve future*, see Felicia Miller-Frank's study. The phonograph is also a crucial technology in Kittler's study.

phonograph) – since his existence is subject to doubt – is God himself:

> isn't it painful to think that if He would just allow the slightest, most humble photograph of Himself – or just permit me, Thomas Alva Edison, American engineer, His creature, to make a simple phonographic record of His True Voice (for thunder has lost most of its prestige since Franklin), *the day after that event, there wouldn't be a single atheist left on the earth?* (24, 788-89)

Edison's desire is to recreate God, that is, project an image of the invisible. Having reconciled himself to the futility of this blasphemous representation, the scientist turns to his second project, the reinvention of Eve.

[A] PHOTOGENIC WOMEN[2]

Photographs of Alicia circulate freely in the text; they remind the reader that it is the model's *image* that Edison and Sowana intend to capture and transpose. The introduction of the first of these photos well precedes the living model's appearance on the scene; in book 2 we behold her image, in book 6 she arrives on Edison's doorstep. Alicia's physical presence is not needed in order to establish her as a personality, all that is required are Ewald's complaints, Edison's suppositions drawn from these complaints, and her photograph. In the passage from book 2, Ewald pulls a miniature Alicia from his pocket, her photographic carte de visite which the Lord carries concealed in a *carnet*. Like all aspiring celebrities, the virtuosa has posed for her carte, thus joining the numerous lesser-known actresses, dance hall girls, and ballet extras who prostituted themselves or who were prostituted through the sale of their images in the nineteenth century. As Elizabeth McCauley notes, "Prostitution and 'furthering one's career' were two sides of the same sou, but a few well-placed photographs could help more than anything to establish a reputation" (104). Alicia is cognizant of this grim reality,

---

[2] A version of this section constitutes part of my article "Snapshots of a Future Eden."

and her photograph, like paper money, is certainly "well-placed" beside her lover/benefactor's skin. Moreover, since cartes de visite were printed in series it may be assumed that others before Ewald have carried a miniature Alicia in their clothing, including her ex-fiancé.

Abigail Solomon-Godeau has exposed the relationship between the carte and female sexuality as fantasized in the nineteenth century (see "The Legs"). Not surprisingly, this rapport is one of fetishism; the photograph would appear to have "developed" on the female body as a symptom of doubt, that provoked by the female form. Solomon-Godeau's analysis of the proximity of the carte to prostitution reinforces the idea that the photograph is historically unthinkable in terms of sexual *indifference*.[3] Alicia, like the Countess de Castiglione discussed by Solomon-Godeau, ultimately retains no control over an image that circulates as an autonomous signifier divorced from its referent. Although her skill at mimicry is complimented ("Some very competent people had told her that . . . she *represented* well" [33, 801]), her representations in no way establish a unique identity for the female model. As the signifying photo is passed from hand to hand and from pocket to pocket, the referent of female subjecthood is lost. Furthermore, photography promotes a progressive distancing of Alicia from her own body; first Ewald and Edison dissociate the two and then her image is denied a connection to her appearance when Edison believes the subject of the carte to be the *Venus de Milo*, not Alicia, "Prodigious! . . . It's nothing less than the famous VENUS of the unknown sculptor!" (56, 826-27). Alicia's carte de visite is (mis)read as that of the *Venus de Milo*, a true nineteenth-century celebrity. Alicia's carte does almost nothing, then, to establish her identity, except in its evocation of a work of art.

Edison's factory for the mechanical reproduction of woman would surpass even that of Disdéri; from the small carte, the American intends to generate an entire race or series of women. A preliminary step in this animation of the snapshot is its enlargement. By means of a crude slide machine, a *lampascope* or magic lantern, Edison projects the photograph which Ewald has handed him onto a screen/canvas:

---

[3] Solomon-Godeau's *Photography at the Dock* also provides insights into photography and sexual difference.

The incandescent ray passed through the imprinted glass by the first of these holes, emerged in full color from the second, which was capped by the inverted cone of a projector – and within a gigantic frame, on a screen of white silk high on the wall, appeared life size the luminous and transparent image of a young woman, a flesh-and-blood statue of the *Venus Victorious*, if such a thing ever lived and breathed in this land of illusions. (58, 829)

The inventor has transformed Alicia's (or the *Venus de Milo*'s) image in three ways: she is now full-size, colorized, and *portraitized*. In this way, Villiers incorporates modern mechanical means of reproduction into an otherwise traditional account of Pygmalion-as-painter. The carte is referred to several more times in the text and stands, paradoxically, as the true *original* image of Alicia, for it allows others to *recognize* her. Edison gives it to his servant so the latter will recognize Alicia upon her arrival, and the inventor recalls the photo when he meets Alicia, "Here was certainly the human original of that amazing photograph which four hours earlier had been projected on the wall screen" (169, 955). Finally, Alicia herself mentions her cartes when she lists the two media that have registered her body (she also possesses, notably, a bust of herself) (176, 963). Again, the blow-up is but an initial image in the succession of representations of woman that *L'Eve future* projects. It is soon joined by other reflections in a photo album that reads as a manuscript detailing the functioning of the android.

Whereas Alicia is photogenic in the sense that she performs well before the spectator, Hadaly is photogenic in that she is both *produced by* and *producing of* light. With Sowana's assistance, Edison, photogeologist as well as inventor and engineer, maps Alicia's form onto Hadaly's armor by means of twenty-four aerial photographs taken during the photosculpture process. These photomaps serve the cartographer in his measurement and assessment of the geology and geography of the female body, for every inch of her body has been photographed. Edison photocopies Alicia onto the android's skeleton, as he says, "I will reproduce this woman exactly, I will duplicate her, with the sublime assistance of Light! . . . *I will duplicate the living woman in a second copy, transfigured according to your deepest desires!*" (64, 836). Alicia is, then, a *passive* model before the photographer, whereas Hadaly proves to be an *active agent* of the photographic process, an active producer of light and its ideality.

As Edison verbally presents his creation to Ewald, Hadaly's body is (orally) "developed." Three of the four mechanical systems that make up Hadaly, the animated photograph, correspond to successive moments in the photographic process: her plastic mediator (armor), her flesh (*carnation*) and her epidermis. Her metallic armor is defined as "The plastic mediator, that is to say the metallic envelope that isolates the inner spaces from the epidermis and the flesh; this is a sort of armor with flexible articulations, within which the interior system is solidly fastened" (129, 908). This metallic envelope is, it would appear, the photographic plate onto which her interior and exterior are joined or fixed. A wide variety of metals were used as photographic plates in the nineteenth century, the earliest being Niépce's tin plates and the copper daguerreotype (the latter was coated with silver). The android is a walking silver plate, "A coat of armor, shaped as for a woman out of silver plates, glowed with a soft radiance. Closely molded to the figure, with a thousand perfect nuances, it suggested elegant and virginal forms" (57, 828). The fixing agent that captures Alicia's image and permanently transposes it onto the plate is a component of the android's *carnation*, which adheres to her metallic shell, "The flesh (or artificial flesh, to call it by its proper name), placed over the plastic mediator and *adhering* to it. When *penetrated by the animating fluid* . . . [*pénétrante et pénétrée par le fluide animant*]" (129, 908; emphasis added). The animating fluid contains, one might say, the fixing chemicals (sodium thiosulphate and potassium bromide were used by early photographers) as well as the developing bath (silver iodide, iron sulphate, and oxalic acid were used) required of the successful emergence of an image. Villiers's mention of Crookes's radiant matter, the "fluide mixte" or magnetic ether that animates the android, is therefore more than a reference to the occultism and mesmerism with which the writer was familiar. It also serves a practical purpose by providing both the light and chemical solution essential to the photographic process.

The final stage or layer of photography that constitutes Hadaly's form is the retouching, the tinting and coloring, of her epidermis:

> The epidermis or human skin, which includes and consists of the coloring, the porosity, the features, the special glitter of the smile, the delicate marks of expression, the exact lip movements of speech, the hair and the entire system of down, the eye assem-

bly, with the associated individuality of the glance, not to speak of the teeth and mouth systems and those of the nails. (129, 908)

While Edison has colorized Alicia's carte by means of a tinted light beam (the exact process is not described), Hadaly will be, it is implied, a product of Charles Cros's three-color synthesis photochromic process, "Photochromic action makes the color permanent [*la sature du ton définitif*]; hence, the Illusion" (151, 935). Edison's coloring glass plates endow artificial skin with human hues and Hadaly's epidermis will be easier to colorize than a landscape photo, Edison argues: "the difficulties of getting lifelike color are much less than when we deal with a landscape, for example. In fact the complexion of our Caucasian race makes use of only two subtly graduated colors, of which we have fairly good technical command; they are pale white and rose" (162, 949). Yet although the Caucasian android is nearly a degree zero of color, she requires the retouching that accompanied the daguerreotype, "A great artist, whom I've inspired with enthusiasm for the special art of revising my phantoms, will come to provide the finishing touches" (152, 936). Indeed, the early years of photography encouraged such cosmetic retouching.[4]

The android's eyes, hair, and smile, which form part of her epidermis, are also products of photography. Edison, who would surely feel at home in the twentieth century, predicts the invention of colored contact lenses, "The addition of color photography gives them [the eyes], besides, a personal touch" (159, 945-46). Next, the foremost hairstylist in Washington is called on to prepare the android's *chevelure*. Edison provides the artist with four peculiar shots of Alicia in which the subject's face is veiled to conceal her identity, "four life-size photographs of a masked head, whose hair and hair styling were to be reproduced" (186, 974). Alicia has begun to replace Hadaly as the female golem in this scene that reminds us of the android's original appearance in a "heavy veil [*voile étouffant*]" (58, 828). As for Hadaly's smile, it is a composite of multiple shots of Alicia's lips in action, which Edison has read, as he tells Ewald,

---

[4] See Schor, "the invention of photography and the widespread popularization of the photographic portrait were almost immediately followed by the inauguration of new techniques of idealization, making it possible to erase unsightly physiognomic blemishes that the camera could not help but register" (*Reading* 49).

"Would you like to see the several dozen photochromic pictures on which are marked the points (precise to several thousandths of a millimeter) where the grains of metallic powder had to be placed in the flesh for the exact magnetic implementation of Miss Alicia Clary's five or six basic smiles? I have them right here, in these boxes" (215, 1011). Contained in boxes and *carnets* exchanged between Edison and Ewald, Alicia's photographs are pieced together – as a puzzle – to produce an exact image of the living woman.

Four other passages that make reference to photography are worth noting. The first is a description of Edison's physique that suggests the superposition of the inventor's photograph and that of Gustave Doré in a stereoscopic representation of the modern genius, who is both *savant* and artist (7, 767). Second, the artificial arm is colorized much like Hadaly's photochromatic epidermis (60, 832). Successive photography is then used to inscribe the gestures which accompany Alicia's recitals onto Hadaly's cylinder (132, 912). And finally, Edison himself assumes the role of photographer when reporters and detectives descend on Menlo Park in an effort to discover the scientist's latest invention. Edison snaps a group photo of these intruders, "As they stood gaping, they were blinded by a tremendous flash of magnesium, set off by the inventor who, in its light, photographed all their hirsute, hispid, hyrcanian mugs" (185, 973). (Edison has evidently perfected the zoom lens.) He subsequently enters a copy of this group portrait as evidence with the police. Photography thus saturates the text; it may appear at any moment as a reminder that a major signifier of the text is the technical object.

Finally, one of the most astounding passages in *L'Eve future* is Edison's description of the *andréide* as a literal photograph. When the inventor instructs Ewald as to the daily care required by Hadaly, the Lord learns that he must attend to his mate as one would to an eternally developing photograph:

> – Does she take baths?
> – But every day, *naturally!* replied the engineer, as if astonished at the question.
> – Ah! said the Englishman, drily. And how is that managed?
> – You know very well that all photographic prints should stay at least several hours in a special solution which reinforces them. (84, 861)

Hadaly will not fade, as an old photograph, if she is renewed regularly in the solution that saturates her epidermis. To summarize, *L'Eve future*'s plot constitutes an exchange of photos: Alicia's carte is replaced by Hadaly, the walking photograph. In both her real and ideal forms, the post-Daguerre woman is a product of the camera's eye.

[B] Maternal Photographs[5]

Baudelaire provides a significant nineteenth-century reading of photography's value as art that rivals his essay on sculpture. The poet's condemnation of the new photographic technology in his 1859 *Salon* is indicative of the widespread doubt that greeted the "industrial art" in its early years (and that has persisted into our own age). His criticisms revolve for the most part around photography's proximity to nature (the real) – what Barthes would later call its ability to render a message without code – at the expense of the beautiful (the ideal), which springs from the artist's imagination. And just as Baudelaire had contrasted (boring) sculpture with (spiritual) painting, he now opposes the photograph and the painted canvas. *Le Public moderne et la photographie* (*The Modern Public and Photography*) (1859) begins, in fact, with a *compte rendu* of the status of *painting* in France.

The tone of Baudelaire's assessment of the modern public's painterly sensibility is one of bitterness and scorn. In words that foreshadow judgments shared by Villiers, Baudelaire describes the French as a nation of doubting Thomases before the true ideal art, "This generation, in fact, both artists and public, has so little faith in painting that it spends its time in seeking to disguise it, to wrap it up in sugar pills like an unpleasant medicine; and what sugar, Great Heavens!" (*Art in Paris* 150). In particular, Baudelaire cites the titles of several paintings as unnecessary sweeteners or veils that distort the spectator's expectations. The writer then moves on to a distinction between beauty and truth, the former being a product of the imagination (the "queen of the faculties"), the latter a mere copy of an abysmal original – nature. The public is drawn to the copy:

---

[5] A version of this discussion of Barthes's *La Chambre claire* appears in my "Picturing the Ideal Feminine: Photography in Nineteenth-Century Literature."

> In matters of painting and sculpture, the present-day *Credo* of the sophisticated, above all in France (and I do not think that anyone at all would dare to state the contrary), is this: "I believe in Nature, and I believe only in Nature (there are good reasons for that). I believe that Art is, and cannot be other than, the exact reproduction of Nature (a timid and dissident sect would wish to exclude the more repellent objects of nature, such as skeletons or chamber-pots). Thus an industry that could give us a result identical to Nature would be the absolute of art." A revengeful God has given ear to the prayers of this multitude. Daguerre was his Messiah. (152)

Art has become synonymous with photography, whereas photography should only serve, Baudelaire argues, as a tool or the painter's aide-mémoire. Finally, it would not be an exaggeration to say that Baudelaire's aversion to photography is in part a product of a painterly paranoia; the public's attraction to the new invention is presented as a "vengeance" and a "conspiracy" against painting.

The bard of modernity's dismissal of photography, spurred by his sense of the incompatibility of photography and the ideal, blinded him to a truth that soon became evident: the painter of modern life is a photographer. Photography's rise has accompanied the expansion of the modern city, a privileged object of the camera's eye. As critics such as Susan Sontag have noted, Baudelaire's *flâneur* is a moving camera, a documentor of modernity's details. This is not to dismiss the parallel growth of the two arts, for Baudelaire's text reveals that photography is rarely thought of without painting at this time. Far from clearly distinguishing themselves as enemies in the nineteenth century, photography and painting mutated and evolved in relation to each other (see Galassi, and Rosen and Zerner). This interdependence is translated in Villiers's description of the projection of Alicia's image. The photograph appears as a *portrait*, "Within a gigantic *frame*, on a *screen* [*toile*] of white silk high on the wall" (58, 829; emphasis mine). The reproducibility of the camera image is, however, the critical difference between photography and painting. This reproduction in turn transforms the portrait into a multiple and transportable image, one that may be projected onto a blank canvas anywhere, at any time.

Baudelaire's late request for his mother's portrait photograph is one instance of his contradictory stance before modernity. This ambivalence concerns the maternal image, or an image that itself *repre-*

sents reproduction. Two years before his death, Baudelaire asks his mother to consider posing for a photographer. Two conditions must be met, however, if the photo is to be a success. First, Madame Aupick should be accompanied to the studio by her son: "I would very much like to have a photograph of you. It is an idea *which now obsesses me*. There is an excellent photographer in Havre. But I fear it is not possible at the moment. *I must be there*. You know *nothing about them* [*Tu ne t'y connais pas*]" (*Letters* 276). Baudelaire's insistence on being present derives from his suspicion that most photographers, even excellent ones, lack a sense of the ideal (a sense which his mother also lacks, it is implied). It may also reveal a need to control his mother's access to her image. Second, the photo must be done in Paris, as Baudelaire continues:

> [You know *nothing about them,*] and all photographers, even the best, have ridiculous mannerisms. They think it a good photograph if warts, wrinkles, and every defect and triviality of the face are made visible and exaggerated; and the HARDER the image is, the more they are pleased. Also, I want the face to measure at least one or two inches. It is only in Paris they succeed in doing what I want, that is, an exact portrait, but having the *softness* [*flou*] of a drawing. But in any case you will think of it, will you not? (*Letters* 276).[6]

Only in Paris will the photograph resemble a drawing, or rather, a black and white *painting*. Baudelaire seeks an ideal photograph, one that denies the perfect mimesis of the apparatus, and an ideal image of his mother – a representation that would erase the warts, wrinkles, and faults of the aged female face.

Strikingly, this association between photography and the maternal reappears in a major contemporary theoretical discussion of photography, Roland Barthes's *La Chambre claire* (*Camera Lucida*). Barthes's study shows that we have not yet done with the association of the maternal and the apparatus, as it interweaves the issues addressed here: maternity, reproduction and technology. A reading of *La Chambre claire* with *L'Eve future* is illuminating, as Barthes's

---

[6] Claude Pichois adds in a note to the Pléiade edition of Baudelaire's correspondance that there is no known (portrait) photograph of Mme Aupick, only a photo of her standing on the terrace of the Honfleur house. Her features in this photo are indiscernable (941n2). The photo that has been retained is indeed *flou*.

text provocatively theorizes the photograph as feminine and endows this technology with a power coveted during the nineteenth century, the power to represent the history of the individual. In this sense, Barthes's text is nostalgic; it looks back to a time, the nineteenth century, when those possessing photographs believed them to render present what they represented, in this case maternal love. Although *L'Eve future* banishes the mother to the sidelines of the text, it allows her to reemerge through its similar insistence on the ability of photography to render maternity present. As such, *L'Eve future* is itself a nostalgic text.

Barthes's Cartesian search for the ontology of the photograph ("So I make myself the measure of photographic 'knowledge'" [9]) ends not with *I photograph, therefore I am*, but rather, *I possess a photo of my mother, therefore I am*. Two thoughts are suggested by this modern *cogito*: first, that photography's strict registration of the past offers a solution to a question raised in the family romance ("Are you my mother?") – it establishes, in other words, genealogical (at least maternal) heritage; and second, that the image of femininity captured by the masculine gaze with the camera is first and foremost a fetish, a substitute for the lost mother. In mourning for his recently deceased mother, Barthes is sorting through photographs when the question of recognition occurs to him, "And here the essential question first appeared: did I *recognize* her?" (65). The quest for knowledge of the photograph-in-itself has become a search for knowledge of the mother. Like Ewald before Hadaly (Hadaly says "Dear friend, don't you recognize me?" [192, 983]), Barthes seeks a reflection – of himself, of his mother, of an ideal feminine essence.

Barthes's recognition is partial; in the photographs he sees bits and pieces of his mother, never her essence:

> According to these photographs, sometimes I recognized a region of her face, a certain relation of nose and forehead, the movement of her arms, her hands. I never recognized her except in fragments, which is to say that I missed her *being*, and that therefore I missed her altogether. It was not she, and yet it was no one else. I would have recognized her among thousands of other women, yet I did not "find" her. I recognized her differentially, not essentially. Photography thereby compelled me to perform a painful labor; straining toward the essence of her identity, I was struggling among images partially true, and therefore totally false. (65-66)

Yet the critic's eye is caught by one photograph of his mother in particular, an image of innocence and wholeness, the photo of his mother as a child, an image which Barthes calls the *Winter Garden*. It would appear that the writer has until this moment been unsure of his mother's very existence (and therefore unsure of her death). But doubt is dispelled as photography assures him that *ça a été*, that he is indeed of woman born.

The authenticity that photography offers is that of lineage, "The Photograph gives a little truth, on condition that it parcels out the body. But this truth is not that of the individual, who remains irreducible; it is the truth of lineage" (103). This association between photography and genealogical time – time measured in generations – endows photography with a power that painting could only approximate. A medium that is inextricably bound up with modern notions of time (in terms of memory and history), photographs will – if allowed to age – ripen as chefs-d'oeuvre.[7] Since photography's invention, Western society has become progressively attached to and dependent on the photographic image; we have even come to see photography as a machine for the mechanical reproduction of aura. And photography's aura, its distance or deferred presence, is anticipated by Hadaly, the animated message without a code.

Like sculpture, photography has been associated by writers and critics with death. The two arts are, after all, those which adorn graves: stone slabs, statues, and photographs of the deceased represent the Other of the living. Photography first erases the model or subject and then effects an artificial resurrection of the dead as souvenir (as Edison resurrects Evelyn through successive photography). This nostalgic move is particular to modernity, "It is a nostalgic time right now, and photographs actively promote nostalgia. Photography is an elegiac art, a twilight art" (Sontag 15). Photography points not to the twilight of the Gods, but to that of humanity. The portrait photograph cannot help but produce a discourse on aging, that is, a history of the individual (in relation to the family), and the photograph album becomes a record of deaths.[8]

---

[7] See Sontag 140, "The depredations of time tend to work against paintings. But part of the built-in interest of photographs, and a major source of their aesthetic value, is precisely the transformations that time works upon them, the way they escape the intentions of their makers. Given enough time, many photographs do acquire an aura."

[8] At the same time that it reveals the truth of aging, photography discloses the

Barthes's remembrance of things past is punctuated with this, the shadowy valley of photography. His confrontation with a photo of his mother is, clearly, a meeting with death. The click of the camera, a "voluptuous" sound, is the Barthesian signifying bar dividing life from death – an aesthetic threshold or purgatory, the subject passes through it from "pose" (life) to "paper" (death). Yet Barthes's choice of a photograph of his child-mother is perhaps a means of using photography's resources to counteract its otherwise uncomfortable revelations; having never *seen* his mother as a child, Barthes is assured by the photo of her proximity to life as well as death. Curiously, what occurs during this search for the lost mother is a gender/age reversal, as Barthes becomes father to his mother. His pregnant metaphor for photography, maternity, is then taken to its logical end when he compares the click of the apparatus, or that which divides the subject – that is, separates him from the mother – to an accouchement, "an image – my image – will be generated [*va naître*]: will I be born from an [*va-t-on m'accoucher d'un*] antipathetic individual or from a 'good sort'?" (11). In fact, the apparatus yields a pleasant photograph of the critic, pleasant because Barthes *recognizes* himself in it. This photo is, need one add, an image of the writer in mourning. The feminine apparatus has given birth to a recognizable image of death. Barthes's father is notably absent from this scenario, as mother and son struggle between life and death, the before and after of the camera's click. Photography democratizes the fabrication of, especially, maternal lineage; now everyone (every man) may claim a purified family tree (on the mother's side, at least).

L'Eve future, while it consistently thwarts the mother's active intervention in the birthing process, remains, paradoxically, a commentary on the family and particularly maternal input in family dynamics. At the opening of *L'Eve future*, Hadaly is a pre-oedipal android, an automaton frozen in the imaginary and depending entirely upon the maternal creator (Sowana) for her identity and means of communication with a (foster or step) father, Edison. *L'Eve fu-*

---

early history of the individual, his or her childhood. The birth of photography is, not surprisingly, closely followed by the invention of psychoanalysis, a delayed investigation into the individual's childhood, "The advent of the new technique ushers in an era of armchair archaeology which will in due time become a 'couch-archaeology,' the recollection in tranquility of traumatic details of the past that is psychoanalysis . . . " (Schor, *Reading* 48).

ture is thus an inverted birth myth: instead of a separation of mother and child it stages a symbiosis of the feminine. Hadaly will never complete her oedipal stage, however; she will not enter the symbolic, for her access to language remains in large part limited to prerecorded messages controlled by Ewald. She will, furthermore, remain one with her mother, as the two permanently fuse as "*une dualité*" towards the end of the text.

That the maternal creator has been a blind spot in many critical analyses of *L'Eve future* is, again, not surprising given the sparse and often confusing information that Villiers provides concerning this character. Sowana is denied, or refuses herself, a stable proper name and a pronoun that would render her present to herself and the reader. There is in effect an apparently concerted effort to dissimulate the mother in *L'Eve future*. Her absence also entails the eclipse of the child as subject, and thus of the family as a central social unit. This is accomplished most forcefully in the substitution of the mother with a male creator who mocks maternity as he brags that his "pregnancy" rivals nature, "Remember, if you will, that mighty Nature herself, with all her resources, still puts some sixteen years and nine months into creating a pretty girl!" (152, 936). In fact, family life seems only *representable* in the text at the expense of the mother and child. Edison's relationship to his offspring, although seemingly affectionate, is extremely minimal and his communication with them is always mediated by one of his inventions, the telephone. The one child who is named – Dash – is also identified with an invention, the morse code. In this way, Edison's family ties are regulated by the technological – his kisses do not require physical presence, only modern machines. As for Mrs. Edison, she is completely absent from the text. Throughout most of the text, Edison is engaged in male bonding with Ewald, but – and this is crucial – male bonding would be impossible without the introduction of the female; the reproduction of woman, not man, is the topic of conversation. The real women of Menlo Park – Edison's wife and Sowana – take a back seat, however, to these (masculine) maternal musings.[9]

---

[9] Bellour's reading of *L'Eve future* as a valorization of the familial through the Edison couple is more than a bit surprising: "Mrs. Edison does not appear in the book, but she is given her symbolic place. This is done – and it is one of the novel's master strokes – by overlapping two couples and two families (the homophony Ed-

The other couple depicted in *L'Eve future*, Edward and Annie Anderson, represents a failed marriage and a dismal family situation. Like Edison's children, the Anderson offspring only appear as absent. Furthermore, it is significant that Edward Anderson's complete rejection of his wife comes when he can see her only as a maternal figure, "he felt that he could see in his wife nothing more than 'the mother of his children'" (107, 884). Anderson opposes maternity and female sexuality; he is repulsed by the former and attracted to an artificial version of the latter. While Evelyn appears to be the cause of the husband and father's downfall, the text suggests that the mother, monstrous in her maternity, is also responsible. Edison argues that the creation of artificial women will preserve marriage and the family by nullifying the courtesan's attractiveness. This modern make over of the family requires, obviously, the exile of real women. Until they are supplemented by facsimiles, mothers will continue to be abandoned and poor. Finally, Sowana's last attachment to life is her children, but she is separated from her offspring because Edison has usurped the mother's authority by "placing" them.

The three unmarried couples of *L'Eve future* – Evelyn Habal and Edward Anderson, Ewald and Alicia, and Ewald and Hadaly – cannot procreate, in each case through the fault of the female partner. When woman is not the absent mother, she is barren. Evelyn uses birth control devices, that is, *artificial* means of preventing conception, and Alicia – a career woman – is not eager to have children. Moreover, there is little chance of her conceiving a child with Ewald, who is disgusted at the thought of intimacy with the bourgeois goddess. Finally, Ewald's ideal woman, Hadaly, will certainly never be a mother. Both real and artificial women are denied reproductive power in *L'Eve future*: they ceaselessly reflect each other in the game of mimicry that produces a monstrous child, Hadaly, but they are incapable of individually mothering natural offspring.

Of course, Ewald himself may be sterile or impotent, given that theories of degeneracy espoused in the latter nineteenth century labeled the aristocracy an infected and dying species. On the other hand, since Ewald is the last in his family line, he may choose con-

---

ison/Anderson can suggest this). Mrs. Anderson is an unhappy double of Mrs. Edison" (125). If Mrs. Edison is "happy," it can only be that silence and absence are the attributes of the happy woman.

sciously to end this line by accepting Hadaly as mate. Villiers is perhaps suggesting that the democratizing photographic machine will replace the aristocracy as society's focus of genealogical concerns. In this way, a "feminized" machine will replace an aristocracy based on male lineage that has grown weak, or effeminate. Photographs proving that one does indeed have a mother would seem to have replaced family names taken from the father.

Despite these erasures of the maternal function from the text, the mother does subversively write herself into the story. As the novel itself can be read as a birth story, so Sowana's illness can be read as a (hysterical) pregnancy. *L'Eve future* stages gestation as hypnosis, during which "the mother infuses the machine" (Doane, "Technophilia" 165). While Sowana sleeps, Hadaly takes form and matures. Alicia's hypnosis then furthers the gestation process – she is frozen as Eve so that Sowana may clone her onto the prenatal Hadaly's metal exterior. Bellour is right to point out that Sowana's input equals and even surpasses Edison's, "[Hadaly is] their co-creation . . . She is at the very source of his capacity to invent" (126). Huet has also stressed the reemergence of the maternal within the seemingly paternity-ridden text. Sowana's gestation period is indeed one of *labor*, but here in the sense of artistic and scientific production. By infusing Edison with her creative powers, Sowana usurps his creation, thereby appropriating the capacity for sublimation denied to women in traditional economies of representation. In fact, Villiers had paved the way for such a "masculinization" of the feminine by denying his female characters their roles as wives and mothers. Sowana does not passively endure her pregnancy, she *labors* as a sculptress and technician, perfecting the form that she will eventually inhabit.

L'Eve future's discourse on the reproduction of works of art is, in the final analysis, a metaphor for the mechanical reproduction of mothering. This groundbreaking text of science fiction is therefore a social commentary, a pamphlet on the state of the family. Absent fathers and mothers, barren women and banished children, all assemble in a story that privileges the marginalia of the family, or those members who subvert the nuclear drama because their relationship to natural reproduction is problematic. Photography is indeed a privileged representational form for this group portrait; it represents the monstrous sterilizing power of the apparatus even as it provides a means of endless cloning. Villiers stops short, however, of the two most monstrous of possible outcomes – a pregnant Hadaly and a photograph of the completed android. Certainty is thus provided that no future monster will exist and that no one will pocket an image of the android as maternal ancestor. Hadaly will not produce Frankenstein's feared "race of devils." Both Shelley and Villiers – and the nineteenth century itself – problematized but in the end skirted the issue of monstrous/mechanical reproduction. Villiers does imply, however, that modern pregnancy is a mechanical process, as the mother (Sowana) is disembodied and in part replaced by the mechanical engineer and his tools. The reproducible artwork *par excellence* sets into motion the sterile fetishization and circulation of the maternal body as *quasi-objets*, two-dimensional referents that proliferate in a never-ending attempt at retroactive matrilineal reconstruction – one might say *in vitro* representation.[10]

[C] MOVING PICTURES

Villiers's innovations on still photography are, I have argued, critical manipulations of a medium whose very significance is in large part grounded in the piecemealing (floating photographic heads and arms) and eventual assembling (developing) of the female body. Edison's most telling or foretelling application of the camera is, however, his use of film or successive photography in yet another imaging of woman. Villiers's prescience (his "pre-science") in this respect is astounding: Edison would indeed be the "father" (or one of the fathers) of the cinema several years after the publication of *L'Eve future*.

Most film historians trace the birth of cinema to 1895, the year in which the Lumière brothers first projected their films to an audience. The audience becomes essential in this search for origins, as Edison's kinetoscope (or peep show) of 1891 has often been bypassed since it allowed for only one spectator. Villiers's "successive

---

[10] Twentieth-century technologies of the image have furthered the artificial construction of matrilineal purity by offering photos of the fetus, a recent addition to the family photograph album. Rosalind Petchesky and others have argued that although these sonographic images may induce 'bonding' between mother and fetus, they reinforce, in the final analysis, a separation between the female body and reproduction which technology promotes by representing the fetus as independent.

photography" allows for an audience and derives, as the technique's name would indicate, from Marey's use in the 1880s of a single camera to produce multiple exposures. The fictional Edison's projector is another variation on the magic lantern previously employed in the reproduction of Alicia's carte. Such a screening may last ten minutes, we are told (117, 897). The film [*ruban*] that Edison uses is, not surprisingly, composed of a series of minute glass plates, given that Eastman's celluloid roll film arrived only in 1889. The real Edison's success followed closely that of the Lumière brothers with the vitascope premiere of "Serpentine Dance," starring Annabelle the Dancer. Both the real and fictive Edisons thus chose the female dancer as the privileged subject of cinema. She was, in fact, the central focus of early cinema, in a continuation of an already established nineteenth-century fascination with the female performer.[11] Evelyn Habal becomes, then, the *first* screen star ever filmed, in this literary prescience of things to come.

Edison's short film – actually two films – allows for the combination of the potentials of the phonograph and photograph. The inventor does privilege the phonograph over the camera as he laments the lost voices and images of history. The utterances that the inventor would have captured include words spoken by God, among them the "sublime soliloquy," "It is not good for man to live alone!" (9, 770). This is the dictum followed by Edison as he hurries to complete Ewald's photogenic mate. But while a male voice – one may assume that Edison hears a male God – compels him to create woman, voice itself is often gendered as feminine in *L'Eve future*. During his recuperation of the past, Edison stresses, however, that the two recording technologies, the phonograph and the camera, must be used in conjunction. His peculiar example of the perfect synthesis of the technologies is an imaginary recording of historic torture scenes, "The camera, aided by the phonograph (they are near of kin), could reproduce both the sight and the different sounds made by the sufferers, giving a complete, an exact idea of the experience" (22, 787). Indeed, a sound track will accompany the actual "torture" film produced by Edison, endowing its now-deceased star, Evelyn, with life. The both male and female voices heard during the screening to be analyzed here reinforce successive

---

[11] On the history of cinema, see Lemagny and Rouillé.

photography's potential for translating and projecting images of the feminine.

Whereas Alicia and Hadaly – the model and copy – are constructed as still portrait photographs, the third female character of *L'Eve future* who participates in the theatrical *mise en abîme* of the text, Evelyn Habal, is animated in a moving picture show. Were it not for Edison's knowledge of this courtesan's disastrous affect on men, the inventor would most likely have neglected a reinvention of woman, in favor perhaps of subsequent musings on the divine Image and Verb. The motivation for the novel's plot is in large part contained, consequently, in the Evelyn Habal sub-plot, the textual tangent that constitutes book 4: *The Secret*. And since this book begins near the exact middle of the novel, Evelyn becomes the central body or image in the text that is Hadaly.

The two clips of Evelyn that Edison has produced and directed and the exhumation of the dancer's belongings conducted during the second screening constitute the essential fragments of evidence entered by Edison during his cross-examination of Ewald on the feminine mystique. A close reading or viewing of these films reveals that cinema is a further application of the photographic fetishizing tool. The cinematic voice in turn reinforces this power of the image by directing and thereby controlling the spectator's (and reader's) gaze. Not only is Evelyn the first screen star imagined by writers, she is imagined in a certain fashion, and this way of projecting the female body would be duplicated in cinematic renditions of film from its beginnings to the present day. Briefly put, Evelyn is a *femme fatale* put on trial by Edison. His short films of her are at once the major pieces of evidence presented in this trial, and a recording *of* the trial, as the reader views the viewing of the film by Edison and Ewald as a short film itself; in other words, Edison and Ewald become characters in the "film" seen by the reader. The narrative strategy of the film within the text thus works to doubly objectify the feminine in the eyes of the reader.

Like Alicia, Evelyn is a performer or re-presenter; she is a ballet walk-on. The cult of the ballerina in nineteenth-century France was a phenomenon that, like that of the early cinema, promoted a fetishization of the female body. By 1850 the ballerina had become synonymous with the prostitute (see Solomon-Godeau, "The Legs"). Thus Evelyn lures the innocent Anderson, who shares a widespread "interest in choreography," into her web of money, sex, and deception. During Edison's analysis of the now deceased dancer, the inventor speaks for the social scientist as he objectively – or so he would have Ewald believe – details woman's machinations. In fact, Edison assumes several paternalistic roles or voices during his discourse, each implying objectivity and omnipotence before the female specimen. He is positivist, "Miss Evelyn Habal thus became for me the subject of a curious experiment" (116, 896) and "I state the facts without passing judgment" (108, 885); detective, "Miss Evelyn Habal! I said to myself. *I wonder what that could possibly be?*" (116, 896); mathematician, "To me Miss Evelyn represented the X of an equation which could, after all, hardly have been more simple since I knew both terms of it: Anderson, and his death" (109, 886); judge (although he also denies playing this part), "I conclude that it's the right of the man as against the woman . . . to inflict a summary execution on her" (113, 891); and statistician:

> Statistics in Europe and America will furnish us with a growing number of similar cases, rising into the tens of thousands every year – identical, or all but identical, with this one . . . The figure of which we speak (and it amounts to fifty-two or -three thousand over the last few years alone) is growing so fast that we may expect it to double within the next few years . . . (108, 885-86)

Scientist, detective, mathematician, judge, and statistician, Edison is the perennial seeker of knowledge whose investigation borders on the perverse, as do all investigations. In this case, Edison's major perversion is voyeurism, for his investigation is visual, "I became obsessed with the idea of analyzing precisely and in detail the nature of those seductions which had been able to disturb such a heart, such senses as his, such a conscience, and bring the man to such a wretched ending" (108, 886). The analyst concludes that *femmes fatales* are not human, but animal (or vegetal, rather, as he compares Evelyn to a poisonous tree). Creatures of base instinct, they are barred from the symbolic and therefore from the protection of society's laws. Edison hints, finally, that Evelyn has suffered a syphilitic death, but the reader may wonder if this judge and jury has not executed his own sentence.

Whether or not Edison literally murders Evelyn remains uncertain; he does, however, symbolically kill her into an image of death. This image, Evelyn's *danse macabre*, is preceded by a clip of the artificial woman in costume. Edison's mode of persuasion is dialectic – he will first show Ewald the positive image and then allow the negative one to impart its full effect. Again, Villiers follows Baudelaire in this dialectical deconstruction of woman: he demonstrates a morbid affinity for the skeletal feminine or representations of woman that oscillate between the ideal and monstrous. Edison will also present now one vision of the artificial sex, now another. This coupling of antithetical images foreshadows Ewald's confusion as he compares Alicia and Hadaly in the garden scene; in both passages the Lord asks Baudelaire's question, "Which is the Real One?"[12]

Ewald first sees Evelyn through Anderson's eyes. Formerly on stage, she is now depicted – as was Alicia's carte – in a framed white cloth (silk for Alicia, canvas for Evelyn). Her image, like Alicia's, is full-size and colorized, "The transparent vision, miraculously caught in color photography, wore a spangled costume as she danced a popular Mexican dance. Her movements were as lively as those of life itself, thanks to the procedures of successive photography . . ." (117, 897). Almost immediately, Evelyn's voice and the sound effects of a tambourine and castanets are added, "Suddenly a voice, rather flat and stiff, a hard, dull voice, was heard; the dancer was singing the *alza* and *ole* of her fandango. The tambourine began to rattle and the castanets to click" (117, 897). This sound emanates from an ornamental addition to the screen's frame activated by Edison, "Edison touched a groove in the black frame and lit a little electric light in the center of the gold rose" (117, 897). The scene thus accomplishes a triple containment of the female body: Evelyn's hollow image is captured on the canvas screen, her voice is "framed" in the border of this canvas, and her cosmetics (her very flesh) are stowed in a drawer.

Ewald falls into Edison's trap as he praises Evelyn's charms, and Edison is now eager to show his second roll of film, the *danse*

---

[12] Baudelaire's prose poem of this title ("Laquelle est la vraie?") may be read as an abridged version of the Evelyn plot of *L'Eve future*. The narrator is mourning at the grave of his lost ideal when her double appears, a hideous "notorious slut" who claims to be the *real* incarnation of his lover. The narrator unsuccessfully argues with the monstous image, "I was furious and replied 'No! No! Never!' – but to emphasize my refusal I stamped on the ground so violently that my leg sank knee-deep into the fresh grave, and like a trapped wolf I found myself caught, perhaps for ever, in the burial-place of the Ideal" (*Poems* 161).

macabre.[13] This is the *real* Evelyn, "On the screen appeared a little bloodless creature, vaguely female of gender, with dwarfish limbs, hollow cheeks, toothless jaws with practically no lips, and almost bald skull, with dim and squinting eyes, flabby lids, and wrinkled features, all dark and skinny" (118, 898). This unretouched image of Evelyn accentuates her faulty form, which the ever-truthful apparatus reveals. Again, a sound track is added, but this time a drunken voice sings an obscene song, "And the whining voice continued to sing an obscene song, and the whole creature continued to dance just like the previous image, with the same tambourine and the same castanets" (118, 898). Edison claims that this is the true Evelyn ("it's the same person; simply, this is the true one" [118, 898]), stripped of her artifices. In fact, Edison has in part obtained this pose through the power of artificial hypnosis, as he has forced Evelyn to play the role of exhibitionist (118, 899). Edison is a Svengali who has mesmerized, we might say drugged, Evelyn in order to undress her – remove her feminine accessories – demystifying her in a pornographic film. The film then continues as Edison displays Evelyn's personal effects to Ewald, commenting on each one. Finally, he terminates the dancing image and singing voice, "The vision disappeared, the singer fell silent; the funeral oration had concluded" (122, 903).

The relationship between Edison and his fabricated visual image of woman is one of voyeurism. Now, voyeurism has been at the foundation of much of film theory since the perversion operates inside and outside of cinematic space (both spectators and male characters are voyeurs). It is also the *original* cinematic perversion, as even early films depicted scenes of looking. According to Laura Mulvey, two types of scopophilia are available to the male spectator confronted with the castration anxiety provoked by the female image: fetishism and voyeurism proper. Fetishism, a denial of castration, is Gortz's choice in Verne's text, for example. Gortz turns La Stilla into an ancestor of Greta Garbo, the twentieth-century female movie star who is idolized as a fetishized product of the male gaze, and who is circulated as a two-dimensional glossy photograph.

Edison, on the other hand, chooses voyeurism, the sadistic side of the scopophilic coin. Voyeurism involves an "investigation" or

---

[13] See John Anzalone's essay on the "danse macabre" in *L'Eve future*.

"demystification" of women like Evelyn Habal (and *"all are, or will be tomorrow (with the help of a little artifice), more or less of her family"* [121, 903]), who are guilty of appropriating the phallus. Femmes fatales are repaid through punishment or salvation, instead of frozen as glossy images. As Mulvey points out in her discussion of Hitchcock, the voyeur/sadist is also representative of law (15). Edison fulfills this role since his films belong to a larger investigation into the nature of femininity. He punishes Evelyn by accusing her of representing the evil castrator, while he urges the death penalty as a more immediate retribution. Finally, whereas fetishism exists "outside linear time as the erotic instinct is focussed on the look alone" (Mulvey 14) – thus Gortz is satisfied with a two-dimensional "still" of La Stilla – voyeurism demands a narrative, "Sadism demands a story, depends on making something happen, forcing a change in another person, a battle of will and strength, victory/defeat, all occurring in a linear time with a beginning and an end" (14). The two films themselves constitute an obvious replay of Edison's defeat of the wicked woman. His menacing monologue – his voice-over – directed at Ewald, continues this sadistic will to persuade from beyond the film's diegesis and the screen's ebony frame.[14]

The director's power over his talking motion picture is twofold – he commands the visual image and the sound recording. Cinema allows and in fact encourages this possession of both the female voice and body. Although film theorists have traditionally privileged the image at the expense of sound, it has become clear to feminist film theorists that the female voice can't be so easily disregarded.[15] Sound motion pictures thus project a double lack upon woman "in the guise of anatomical deficiency and discursive inadequacy" (Silverman 1). Edison's own films, although not talkies, en-

---

[14] I should admit my perhaps uncomfortable application of the terminology of dominant narrative film theory to a primitive set of shorts which sing but do not converse. What I wish to show is that Villiers's fantastic documentary predicts not only the birth of cinema, but the birth of a certain *kind* of cinema. My reason for using this discourse also springs from the richness of its terminology. Finally, while Edison's films are not talkies, they do presumably involve the synchronization of the female singing voice and her image.

[15] See Kaja Silverman's discussion of the importance of the female (especially maternal) voice in dominant cinema. Feminist film theory and criticism is extensive; the work of Doane and Silverman has had the greatest impact on this discussion. See also Roy Armes's article on documentary film and the voice-over.

gage both the female voice and body in a deconstruction of femininity. During both screenings, the inventor's sober voice-over draws attention away from Evelyn's drunken song and clanging castanettes. The contrast between Edison's controlled and controlling sober (male) voice and Evelyn's seemingly uncontrollable and drunken (female) voice is startling. Edison becomes commentator and ventriloquist [16] as he first praises the dancer's appearance (tongue in cheek, of course) and then delivers a biting lecture, which begins "*Ecce puella*," on the craftiness of women like Evelyn. A true photojournalist or documentary filmmaker, Edison continues to spew out statistics, "Read the thousands of newspapers which every day and in every land repeat the same story and you will see that, far from inflating my figures, I am understating them" (118, 899), all the while inserting his statistics into a dramatic narrative.

As Doane has shown, the documentary voice-over, traditionally a male prerogative, implies a command of knowledge and interpretive powers:

> It is its radical otherness with respect to the diegesis which endows this voice with a certain authority. As a direct form of address, it speaks without mediation to the audience, by-passing the 'characters' and establishing a complicity between itself and the spectator – together they understand and thus place the image. It is precisely because the voice is not localizable, because it cannot be yoked to a body, that it is capable of interpreting the image, producing its truth. ("Voice" 42)

Edison's voice is localizable, but the comparison still holds if we read his role as that of the presenter (ancestor of the documentary voice-over) whose presence was all-important (see Armes). *L'Eve future*'s second feature film clearly allots different spaces to the male and female cinematic voice. Edison invents Evelyn's biography, and the subtext becomes the origin of the novel's plot, whereas the female voice endures diegetic containment as Evelyn's voice remains framed and confined by the song's lyrics. Furthermore, the male documentary voice continually threatens the very repre-

---

[16] Beizer identifies the nineteenth-century narrator as a ventriloquist who would speak the hysteric's words. Certainly, Edison and Villiers can be identified as two of these narrators who in this scene speak for or over the singing Evelyn.

sentability of the female image itself. The inventor of the phonograph, that is, of the voice itself, displaces the female voice, supplants it, in favor of his own verbal dissection of the image. Finally, Edison's statements determine the spectator's understanding, his way of *seeing* female nature. This is especially true in Edision's theatre, as Ewald is the one and only spectator.

The voyeur's escape from the female image – an image that he himself has constructed – thus entails the defilement and defacement of woman as object of the camera and her erasure as potential cinematic spectator. In the end, the reader is made to view these films as Ewald does at Edison's instigation: as a sadistic voyeur.

CHAPTER 5

EARLY IMAGES OF PSYCHOANALYSIS

The walls of Freud's consulting room at Berggasse 19 displayed the bibelots, decorative symptoms, or icons of the psychoanalytic movement. They included a copy of André Brouillet's painting *La Leçon clinique du Dr. Charcot*, photographs of Freud's family and friends, a collection of reproductions of ancient figurines and a copy of the ancient bas-relief known as the *Gradiva*. Brouillet's canvas depicts one of Charcot's theatrical demonstrations of hysteria at the Salpêtrière Hospital – it represents, therefore, a possible origin of psychoanalysis, its primitive scene: hysteria staged before the male medical gaze as a bona fide disease. Juxtaposed with Freud's photographs, *La Leçon* recalls the infamous "photograph albums" of the "family" of female hysterics who were systematically posed before the apparatus during Charcot's reign. Further along this syntagm of the Freudian museum, one finds a cast of *Gradiva* – the stone woman with the peculiar gait and a female character in a fictional account interpreted by Freud as a successful analytic cure. Images of the feminine are thus inscribed onto the very walls of Freud's study, as bas-reliefs and photographic portraits.

The reproduction of sculptural and photographic images is a method of immobilizing the feminine in order to examine it in detail and ultimately reconstruct an idealized version of woman. Charcot's photographs and Freud's fetish for the sculptural are historical symptoms of this process. Psychoanalysis, the discourse that marks the culmination of nineteenth-century ideologies of woman and heralds twentieth-century fantasies of the feminine is itself foreshadowed in Villiers's timely portrayal of tomorrow's Eve as a symptomatic icon. Elements of both Charcot's contemporary and

Freud's future insights echo throughout *L'Eve future*, and reveal in retrospect the dependence of early psychoanalysis on the image of woman.

[A] TECHNOLOGIES OF THE FEMININE

Michel Foucault's discourse on the birth of sexuality in the late eighteenth and nineteenth centuries in *La Volonté de savoir* (*The History of Sexuality*) posits four institutions that represent specifically bourgeois articulations of the relations between power, knowledge and the body: pedagogy, medicine, psychiatry, and demography. These strategies give form to four corpora or prototypes of the bourgeois body: the masturbatory child, the hysterical woman, the adult pervert and the reproductive (Malthusian) adult. Together, these "technologies of sex" are subsumed under the larger dominant narrative of *scientia sexualis*. Medicine, psychiatry, economics and criminology, these are the nineteenth century's technologies of applied sexuality. Futhermore, according to Foucault, the foundation of modernity's *scientia sexualis* is a history of the confession (*l'aveu*). *L'Eve future* is the record of Ewald's confession of his relationship to desire to Edison, and thus serves as a prime example of a literary transcription of an imagined technology of applied sexuality.

Technology in the Foucauldian sense refers to the effects or products of the bourgeois *machine à fabriquer la sexualité* (Hadaly is a "machine à fabriquer l'idéal") – the institutions, strategies, and models of behavior mentioned above. But the term may also be interpreted quite literally as an allusion to the applied sciences or industry. The adoption of this word in a history of nineteenth-century (re)production of sexuality is significant, for the rise of technology both accompanies and contributes to the birth of the body as a sexual representation. In short, technology is itself a technology of sex. I want to propose, then, that technology be afforded a prominent place in a list of empowering bourgeois discourses. In particular, I am interested in the application of the technological to the "hysterization" of woman, a process that requires the participation of the medical apparatus among a wide range of mechanical instruments. The bourgeois (aesthetic) strategies of artifice of photography and sculpture (in its bibelot form) must be appended to an inventory of technologies of sex, as, specifically, tools of hysterization.[1] The application of these two arts/technologies is fundamental to the construction of the female body as image in the nineteenth century – this is, again, the significance of *L'Eve future*. Sculpture in particular is a crossover technology that, while embedded in aesthetic tradition, has been appropriated by technology as an implement of reproduction. As for photography, its status as both technology and art makes it a privileged tool for imaging the female corpus as a technology of sex.

A technology of technology that addresses the construction of female sexuality necessitates a gendering of both Foucault's reading of the modern body and Serres's entropic model of the industrial. Feminist critics have begun just such a revision, especially in the case of Foucault's outline of hysterization, a process that situates the female body as the very site of medical production. Teresa de Lauretis has proposed that gender and sexuality be considered as connected factors in all technologies of representation, including cinema, literature, and theory itself.[2] Kittler's insight, that technologies are not "productive" of meanings but are the context in which "meaning" may (or may not) be assigned, is also crucial here. That Villiers's ideal woman is a machine – a product of metallurgy and electricity – is indicative of a hysterization of the machine as feminine in the nineteenth century, and of the ability of hysteria to develop *as a discourse*. The clinical apparatus, which includes the camera, is a privileged machination of medicine in this mechanization of the female body. This mechanization reaches beyond medicine, furthermore, to include all desiring engines (or engines of desire) of nineteenth-century sexuality.

Reproductive technologies, a fourth bourgeois means of supervising sexuality, are also, of course, gendered as feminine. Although the male's relationship to reproductive issues – like the female's – has been regulated according to the family alliance, corporeally speaking childbearing is "written" onto the female body. In the twentieth century surrogate motherhood, artificial insemina-

---

[1] Beizer's study addresses what she calls the "hystericization of culture" in nineteenth-century France.
[2] See de Lauretis, *Technologies of Gender*, especially chapter 1. For a discussion of Foucault's skirting of the question of gender, see Schor, "Dreaming Dissymmetry."

tion and *in vitro* fertilization are reproductive behaviors to be valorized or repressed. The ambivalence and anxiety that surrounds these technologies that find their origin in the nineteenth century's discourse on demography is indicative of a broader bourgeois will to control and manipulate proliferation, a strategy that assumes and promotes the feminization of the procreative machine. The commodification of the *objet d'art* has not escaped this same type of process. That discourses on sculpture and photography often disclose a bedrock of concern with maternal reproduction strongly suggests that representation, technology and the feminine are intimately allied in the nineteenth-century unconscious and have continued to dominate twentieth-century *scientia sexualis*.

Both photography and sculpture played a role in the early history of psychoanalysis and therefore in the hysterization of woman in the nineteenth century. Furthermore, the hysterization of woman that pervades the medical and later psychoanalytic discourses of the nineteenth century provides in large part the ideological foundation of *L'Eve future*. The text may be read, in fact, as a case study of several incurable hysterics who are replaced by an ideal female fabrication who, one may assume, will display no signs of a nervous disorder. Edison, Villiers's engineer, philosopher, inventor, and, finally, *doctor*, speaks for the nineteenth-century medical corpus that appropriated the female body as its object of analysis. He is a *hysterisizer* of women, as Alicia, Evelyn, Sowana and even Hadaly – especially Hadaly – are presented as effects or symptoms of his will to produce the feminine. And finally, Edison's use of photography and sculpture in the creation of a new Eve also aligns him with the early history of psychoanalysis, for Charcot the would-be painter was a closet photographer and Freud was a repressed sculptor of woman.

The hysteric comprises one quarter of Foucault's modern body. In turn, hysterization is a triple endowment of the female body. Woman is, first, an object of analysis reduced to her sexuality, "the feminine body was analyzed – qualified and disqualified – as being thoroughly saturated with sexuality." Second, her body is a specimen for medical observation, "it was integrated into the sphere of medical practices, by reason of a pathology intrinsic to it." And third, her body is codified as maternal:

> it was placed in organic communication with the social body (whose regulated fecundity it was supposed to ensure), the fam-

ily space (of which it had to be a substantial and functional element), and the life of children (which it produced and had to guarantee, by virtue of a biologico-moral responsibility lasting through the entire period of the children's education): the Mother, with her negative image of "nervous woman," constituted the most visible form of this hysterization. (Foucault *History* I: 104)

L'Eve future presents four images of nineteenth-century hysteria. Sowana, the "mother" of Hadaly, is perhaps the most prototypical of these nervous women, since Villiers's text reads as a case history of the somnambulist. She also answers to Foucault's archetypal hysteric: the nervous woman who is also a maternal figure. Annie Anderson the mother and Any Sowana the *malade*, fusing as one, represent the two sides of the mother: the negative nervous woman and the maternal image. They produce, therefore, an example of the most "visible" form of hysteria.

Both Edison and Ewald mention hysteria several times in the course of their discussion of Alicia. Ewald complains that Alicia displays the hysterical symptom of uncontrollable, hence pathological, verbal repetition. She is like all "maniaques" who cannot help but exude the poison of hysteria through incessant positivist utterances, "[So that] they soon acquire the lucrative and mechanical habit of continually pronouncing these vocables – and this practice before long steeps them thoroughly in the mindless hysteria with which the words are soaked" (40, 809). Speech does not offer Alicia access to an empowering symbolic, but rather condemns her to meaningless theatrical outbursts. Repetition, the ability to mime or represent, is, again, the trademark of the hysteric. But whereas all the women of *L'Eve future* are implicated in the acting out of the nervous woman, Alicia has surpassed even the hysteric, as Ewald notes during his recital of her case history:

> Believe me, my dear doctor, I haven't come to your consulting room in order to describe to you, under the simpleminded supposition that my affliction is unique, some trivial case of hysterical dementia, more or less banal, such as one can find written up in all the medical textbooks. The case is of a different and much more astonishing order of physiological difficulty; you may take my word for that. (31, 798-99)

Like Edison, Ewald assumes the discourse of the doctor. He then proceeds to diagnose Alicia as *more* than hysterical. Her surplus of illness is, in fact, the excess that attracts Doctor Edison to her case. She is a "hybrid" hysteric who cannot be cured and must therefore be replaced.

Evelyn Habal, whom Edison views as a specimen for laboratory experimentation, is characterized as a gaseous, thermodynamic being who emits the vapors of hysteria. Hysteria itself was at one time referred to as *vapors*, since it was thought to be caused by the exhalations of bodily organs. Edison warns Ewald of women like Evelyn and "the slow hysteria which distills from them" (112, 890), "ces 'évaporées'" (890). This feminine substance in turn infects the *femme fatale*'s male spectators with contagious hysteria, as they become "a melancholy collection of hysterical ninnies" (109, 887). The ethers of hysteria – reminiscent of magnetic and "radiant" fluids – were, in fact, privileged signifiers and inducers of hysteria in the nineteenth-century clinic. Ether, amyl nitrate, chloroform, bromides, and even tobacco smoke, to name but a few, were the fumes used at the Salpêtrière as stimulators of the hysteric's sense of odor, inducing delusions. They are, at the same time, indicators of feminine fumes, or an *odor di femina*.[3] Edison mentions such experiments twice: first he declares that Hadaly will respond to Ewald as a hysteric under the influence of "a flask of cherry water hermetically sealed" (143, 924-25); later, describing the "third fluid," he relates it to a drug that induces convulsions, sneezes, cries and vomiting in the hysteric (213, 1008-09). The simple manometer used by Cros's protagonist as a measure of female vapors is replaced in *L'Eve future* by an elaborate recreation of Evelyn's post-mortem odiferous presence.

L'Eve future's references to hysteria, a popular catch-all phrase for female maladies in the nineteenth century, are certainly broad enough so as to include all four examples of woman in the text. This is true even of Hadaly, who at first appears to be Ewald's salvation or relief from the hysteric's unbearable repetitions. Yet Hadaly's repertoire is itself a never-ending litany of performances – bearable only because they have been staged and recorded by man. Edison indicts all women as hysterics when he says of Alicia, "this woman *would be the absolute feminine ideal for three-*

---

[3] See Didi-Huberman 210-13. Drugs were also employed as stimulators of hysterical states. As a result, many patients died addicted to ether, morphine and alcohol.

quarters of modern humanity!" (44, 814), and, in reference to Evelyn, that all women *"are, or will be tomorrow (with the help of a little artifice), more or less of her family"* (121, 903). The label "hysteric" is, paradoxically, both a contemporary condemnation and a positive designation of the feminine. Although Villiers makes reference to existing medical treatments of hysteria (inhalations, hypnosis, drugs), and although Sowana's story is, clearly, a case history, *L'Eve future* offers for the most part a layman's view of the nervous woman – a view that most readers could recognize. In fact, it was not until Charcot that hysteria was defined as a specific form of nervous disorder with its own symptoms and etiology. Yet "hysteria" remained, even after Charcot, a popular literary denotation for the representative and even ideal bourgeois woman. As Edison bluntly says, *most* men would appreciate Alicia's symptoms.[4]

In an obituary that Freud wrote upon Charcot's death in 1893, the former student distinguished the French doctor's novel approach to illness as follows, "He was not a reflective man, not a thinker: he had the nature of an artist – he was, as he himself said, a 'visual,' a man who sees" (3: 12). In fact, two of Charcot's works address the representation of disease and dementia in art (see Charcot and Richer). Charcot is a prototype of the nineteenth-century clinician whose medical gaze provided a window onto and a means of entry into the patient's – here the hysteric's – body, that clinician described by Foucault in *The Birth of the Clinic*. But again, Charcot enters and observes *as an artist*, as one who both detects and *produces* forms. Often accused of artifice, of being theatrical (as Freud tells us), Charcot's staging of hysteria was a public spectacle that may be opposed to Anna O's "private theatre." Whereas Freud positioned himself as the interpreter of an "other scene," Charcot assumed the role of scenographer or set director of the scene before his eyes (see Didi-Huberman 133). Charcot thus integrates, in his relationship to hysteria, the arts that come into play in *L'Eve future*: painting, theatre, photography, and sculpture. Whereas his keen sense is sight, that of Freud is hearing, in the sense of understanding (*l'entendement*), "Charcot sees, Freud will hear" (Heath, *Sexual*

---

[4] The fact that Ewald is an aristocrat does not invalidate a reading of *L'Eve future* as a *bourgeois* manual for the reproduction of sexuality. Ewald's possible sterility and the fact that he is attracted to apparently barren women may be interpreted as a progressive exclusion of the upper class from procreative technologies.

38). Yet Freud's interpretations go beyond the audible, as psychoanalysis's papa returns several times in his work to sculptural representations. The status of the image in the work of Charcot and Freud – these pivotal fabricators of the feminine – reveals an undercurrent of psychoanalytic iconography in *L'Eve future*, a narrative that also recounts the construction of woman as image.[5]

[B] Aura Hysterica

During Charcot's thirty years at the Salpêtrière, the women's asylum become much more than a significant locus in the medical history of hysteria – it represented, in the words of Didi-Huberman, a veritable chapter of art history (10). Charcot the visual not only defined and investigated hysteria at the Salpêtrière, he staged it repeatedly in his *Leçons du mardi*, which were transcribed by his students and read as one-act plays. He also directed the recording of hysterical productions in the form of photographs and wax casts. Two production sites of the nineteenth-century artist were thus represented at the clinic: the wax museum (called, at the Salpêtrière, the "Musée Charcot") and the photography studio. The latter produced three volumes of the *Iconographie photographique de la Salpêtrière* (1876-77, 1878, and 1879-80), and the *Nouvelle iconographie photographique de la Salpêtrière* (1888-1918).[6] In his tribute to Charcot, Freud called the Salpêtrière "that museum of clinical facts" (3: 13); it was, however, a museum of images, too, where poses were frozen, exhibited, and labeled. The wax museum, with its full-size and partial casts of hysterics (often the paralyzed appendage was reproduced alone) is a revealing commentary on the relationship between sculpture, medicine, and the feminine. Reminiscent of the Spitzer Museum, a latter nineteenth-century traveling exhibition of wax male and female body parts, this modeling laboratory is reflected in Edison's collection of anatomical simula-

---

[5] Jann Matlock and Janet Beizer's studies of hysteria and the novel in the nineteenth century are superb and detailed analyses of the relationship between the disease and narrative. Neither discusses *L'Eve future*, but their respective works shed considerable light on Villiers's novel.

[6] The early volumes were edited by D.-M. Bourneville; the photographer was Paul Régnard. The *Nouvelle iconographie* was edited by Charcot, Gilles de la Tourette, and Paul Richer and included the photographs of Albert Londe.

tions – represented by the artificial arm of *L'Eve future*.[7] The Salpêtrière's *service photographique* is, however, surely one of the most impressive examples of a concerted and systematic containment of woman as art and technical object in the nineteenth century. Charcot's use of photography is a means of establishing a visual history, or genealogy, of hysteria; once again, technology interprets the feminine as an instrument for the production of heredity.

Among the numerous female hysterics who were paraded before the camera and whose images were published in the family albums of the Salpêtrière, one in particular stands out as a model specimen. Augustine, also referred to as Louise, X, L, and G – thus representing a plurality of hysterics but no one in particular – arrived at the institution in 1875 at the age of fifteen. Her contribution to the visual history of hysteria corresponds in many ways to Alicia's role in *L'Eve future*. Augustine's gestures, labeled according to the stage of hysteria represented – "hystéro-épilepsie," "tétanisme," and "attitudes passionnelles," to name a few – were assembled in series of successive images, thus providing an almost cinematic record of the metamorphic hysteric. She is, like Alicia, the model for a prototype as photography transforms her into the ideal hysteric. It was not until 1880 that this photojournal was complete, complete because her escape from the Salpêtrière marks the end of her posing and thus the end of her story.[8] Nothing is known of Augustine's subsequent life beyond the parameters of the institution and the photographic studio. The last detail we possess of her story is highly significant, however: Augustine escaped confinement to a cell – her punishment, we might say, for no longer posing well – disguised as a man. This masquerade marks her refusal to submit to the apparatus (male hysterics did not appear in the series until 1888). The transvestite's avoidance of the camera's eye comes at the expense of her gender identity, yet Augustine's femininity had itself been thrust upon her to a certain extent. Her final recital, as a man, was in a sense her best performance and, paradoxically, her most sincere attempt at self-representation.

---

[7] The Spitzer exhibit also included simulated surgical operations/mutilations. See Heath, *The Sexual Fix*, "two hands, wrists, cuffed and jacketed, hold down a woman's body, while two more cut into her womb . . . " (24n).

[8] It also marks the end of the *Iconographie photographique*, although the interruption of publication was not to my knowledge directly related to Augustine's departure. For Augustine's story and photos, see Bourneville and Régnard, *Iconographie* 2: 123-86.

Through photographic reproduction, Augustine became a signifier for the now defined "hysteria." Indeed, the photography studio of the Salpêtrière is the democratizer of the hysteric with Augustine as its *Marianne*, immortalized in a handbook or declaration of hysteria as a true (female) malady. The camera thus functions, in this bourgeois appropriation of the female body, as an equalizer of the feminine. All women, it is implied, are hysterics to some degree. All aspire to and may attain the success represented by Augustine, "chef-d'oeuvre" of hysterics (Didi-Huberman 119). Thus the hysteric joins the ranks of those who wrested self-representation from the upper class in the nineteenth century (including the courtesan, dancer and actress). There is, indeed, something of the Countess of Castiglione in Augustine – so eager to pose, so eager to please. Yet in the end photography fails to reveal the causes or stories behind the hysteric's state. The medium that registers a message without a code merely reflects the hysterical symptom, a message that will not be decoded until the arrival of Freud. Charcot's approach to hysteria remains purely visual as symptoms, like photographs, are incorporated into medicine as pure representations.

The elevation of hysteria to the status of neurological disorder endows the illness and those who suffer from it with (medical) authority. In turn, the process of hysterization, whereby technologies concur in a reproduction of female symptoms, is an authorization of the female body as a privileged site of modern aura. By "modern aura" I mean that distance that is replicated by the photograph, the cinema, and other mechanical subversions of presence. Bourgeois aura is, certainly, a decay of the uniqueness of the traditional (non-reproducible) work of art. Yet at the same time, mass reproduction produces its own form of distance – not that between an original work and its spectator, but the distance of Lacanian desire, or that which cannot be satisfied. Augustine the actress is doubly unapproachable because her relationship to a "self" is always already suspect. She represents the distance and void of the modern theatre *vedette* described by Chambers ("L'Ange"). Rather than emitting an aura steeped in cult value, Augustine and Hadaly depend for their value on the multiple investments of their spectators (doctors, lovers). Desire in the modern sense is a side effect or excess of the longing for the unattainable Other, it is that which can be confronted only in fetishized *petit 'a*'s, the replicated appendages of the female body. A consequence of this fragmented aura is, therefore, the impossibility of encountering a whole body. All that may be grasped are the partial objects, the limbs and features, of the posing woman. The *Iconographie photographique* and *L'Eve future* are commentaries on this loss of the aura of wholeness and uniqueness. They narrate the emergence of the forever postponed aura of the artificial.

Interestingly enough, the word *aura* is implicated in both the history of photography and the genealogy of the hysterical attack. First, *aura* may refer to an atmosphere or appearance apprehended by the senses; for example, aromas are auras of the sense of smell. Second, *aura* is a medical term used to describe the pre-hysterical state. *Webster's* gives us: "a subjective sensation (as of voices, colored lights, or crawling and numbness) experienced before an attack of epilepsy, migraine, or certain other nervous disorders." Charcot labeled this necessary prerequisite to an authentic hysterical fit the *aura hysterica*. A typical account of this aura is the following (taken from Augustine's case history):

> *Aura.* – It is composed of the following phenomena: 1. an ache situated in the right ovary (ovarian hyperaesthesia); 2. [sic] the sensation of a ball rising to the epigastric region (epigastric knot); 3. cardiac palpitations and laryngeal constriction (third knot); 4. finally, cephalic disturbances (throbbing in the temple and the anterior of the right parietal, hissing in the right ear). (Bourneville 2: 129, my translation)

That the "rise" of aura in the hysteric's body involves a shift from ovaries to "voice-box" to head should not come as a surprise to anyone familiar with nineteenth-century medical mappings of significant female corporeal zones.

Third, *aura* indicates a phenomenon of light (a glow or radiation) that the camera may uncannily register as visible. A certain Doctor Baraduc, a fin-de-siècle neurologist and photographer, developed a "radiographic" process whereby the photographed subject's very "soul" was captured as radiant matter or vital fluid.[9] Many of Baraduc's photographic auras were, not surprisingly, those of Charcot's patients. In this way photography, the technical art,

---

[9] On Baraduc, See Didi-Huberman 89-97. The cause of this phenomenon is still not clearly established.

was manipulated as a tool of access to an arcane world of radiant beings such as Hadaly and Sowana, souls or auras of a distant world (as *aura* also signifies "astral body"). Aura is photography become revelation, and the choice of hysterics as subjects for these photos reveals their mystical significance. Photography would thus provide visual evidence for an alliance suggested in Charcot's work: the hysteric as saint (the crucifixion pose was popular among hysterics, or at least among their photographers). Radiography is, finally, a further instance of the photographic containment of the hysteric, this time of her very essence. Clearly, what can be seen at first glance – the hysteric's physical symptoms – is not perceived as valid enough evidence for the existence of these women. What needs to be revealed is that which cannot be seen, that is, that which remains invisible to all eyes but those of the medical apparatus.

Augustine is posed in the *Iconographie photographique* as a modern incarnation of Saint Teresa of Avila. Whereas the sixteenth-century mystic is anesthetized in a sulpture by Bernini, the nineteenth-century hysteric is hypnotized in a series of photographs. Indeed, Bernini's "The Ecstacy of Saint Teresa" is contained and reproduced in the images of Augustine, who reflects and mimes the saint. One indication of this ancestry of modern representations of the feminine is the obvious "sculpturalization" of the photographs of Augustine – her institutional clothing, especially, is retouched to resemble statuary folds. To paraphrase Lacan, one has only to go and look at the *Iconographie photographique*'s reproductions of Augustine's "attitudes passionnelles" to know it: the passionate saint is the model for the mass reproduction of the hysteric. Furthermore, Bernini's cupid, who aims an arrow at Teresa's vagina, is mirrored by Charcot's stance before the hysteric, during which the doctor replaces the arrow with a pointer aimed at the patient's ovaries (these are the infamous "ovarian compressions"). Charcot draws, therefore, on two artistic forms in his effort to subdue the feminine. He will immobilize the hysteric as, alternately, a hypnotized and hypnotic statue, and a retouched photograph. This process leads to the mutual modification of the two arts as they converge in the production of a fetishized, fragmented, and reconstituted female body.

One of Charcot's preoccupations was the preservation of disease in sculptural form, specifically in wax casts. Yet the use of hypnosis at the Salêtrière perhaps reflects to a greater degree this determination to petrify woman. The mesmerized woman is idealized as a statue, just as Ewald would accept Alicia if only she would keep quiet and close her eyes in an imitation of the *Venus de Milo*. Charcot controls the periodic animation of the hysteric's body parts as his verbal commands and adroit pointer induce various contractions and paralyses. Hypnosis is not, however, the doctor's sole means of provoking immobility. At times, electrical impulses (*faradisation*) are applied in an effort to localize desired expressions. This artificial prolongation of the pose allows the photographer – whose procedure was often lengthy – to accomplish his task, as Charcot tells us:

> The physiognomy stays immobilized in catalepsy, and the same for the posture and the gesture that have accompanied it. The subject finds himself thus transformed into a *sort of expressive statue, immobile model* representing with a keen truth the most diverse expressions and which artists could surely turn to account.
>
> The immobility of postures obtained in this way is eminently favorable to photographic reproduction. (Quoted in Didi-Huberman 284. Emphasis added and trans. mine)

Yet another means of posing the hysteric was to, literally, *repress* her. Models who could not maintain their positions were strapped to a head-restraint, again in the name of art. In this way, Albert Londe notes, photos were obtained of particular facial features:

> one must use it [the head support] when the patient can't stay immobile and when the lack of light prevents the taking of a snapshot. It is the same when one works very closely and desires to make enlargements of the head or parts of it: the eyes, the mouth, the nose or the ears. (Quoted in Didi-Huberman 278, trans. mine)[10]

For serious cases – those hysterics who could not stand straight or walk – Londe advises the use of a support bracket. The patient is literally suspended from her head and arms, hanging from the photographer's gallows.

---

[10] Albert Londe was director of the photographic service at the Salpêtrière. His *La Photographie médicale* discusses in detail the techniques used to photograph patients. Of course, the use of supporting mechanisms was commonplace in the early years of photography and not limited to medical photography.

Although they are arts with different aesthetic traditions, photography and sculpture work towards a common goal – the positioning of woman as a symptom of male desire. The pose assumed by the hysteric, a direct consequence of hypnosis, drugs, and mechanical restraint, attains archetypal status in the passionate attitudes of Augustine and Saint Teresa. Hadaly too is constructed as a product or reinforcement of male desire. Like Charcot, Edison privileges the photography and sculpture laboratories of his female factory. While electricity and metallurgy *appear* to be the crucial technologies of this nineteenth-century factory, there is in reality a significant aesthetic foundation for the products that Edison would put on the market. Photography and sculpture, metamorphosed as instruments of the scientist, are privileged technologies of reproduction that underlie and sustain the modern proliferation of the feminine.

[C] Saxa Loquuntur!

There exists a genealogical link between the photograph albums of the Salpêtrière and the presence of a repressed sculptural fetishism in the works of Freud, the modern technician of female sexuality. One of photography's significant effects is that it provides evidence of ontogenetic history; the family album contains the ruins of an individual ancestry. Sculpture, on the other hand, reveals a phylogenetic heritage; stone ruins tell the story of Western civilization. Freud applies phylogenetic representation to the ontogenetic recovery of the individual's origins in his oft-cited archaeological metaphor for psychoanalysis. As early as the *Studies on Hysteria*, he advocates the excavation of repressed material, "This procedure [free association] was of clearing away the pathogenic psychical material layer by layer, and we liked to compare it with the technique of excavating a buried city" (2: 139). The analyst encourages the patient to talk away the strata of trauma that coat the hysterical mind. In the same way, the archaeological dig involves the chiseling away of recent debris to reveal an earlier "true" civilization.

The metaphor is found throughout the Freudian *opus*. Notably, Freud compares the female pre-oedipal stage that he outlined late in his life in *Female Sexuality* to an unexpected archaeological discovery, "Our insight into this early, pre-Oedipus, phase in girls comes to us as a surprise, like the discovery, in another field, of the Minoan-Mycenean civilization behind the civilization of Greece" (21: 226). The analyst who digs deep enough will find, beneath the Greek *Oedipus*, a feminine myth, and the psychoanalytic quest is a quest for origins – for the buried stone foundation of an initial structure. More than a metaphor, however, the archaeological image is played out in two Freudian texts that discuss ancient civilizations and their stone icons, *Delusions and Dreams in Jensen's 'Gradiva'* (1907) and *The Moses of Michelangelo* (1914). Both of these texts also posit the origin of the feminine: in the first work the female foot becomes signifier of sexual difference, in the later the male foot becomes a symbol of the incest taboo, or the denial of the mother as feminine.

That Freud was a prolific collector of ancient statuettes may be interpreted as a fetishistic manifestation of this archaeological penchant.[11] These symptoms of a personal figurine fetish are signs or remains of an early emphasis on the image in psychoanalysis, evinced in Freud's desire to read the hysteric's body as an example of plastic representation. Freud's work around the turn of the century constitutes, in effect, the record of a passage from image to text, just as Villiers's text records the failure of the image to incarnate the ideal feminine, but a successful verbal account (a talking cure?) of this modern problem. In renouncing hypnosis for free association, Freud replaced a Pygmalion complex concerning his patients with a collection of miniature reproductions, his figurines or bibelots. Charcot the visual interpreted the hysterical body in terms of imagery; Freud's free association will rely solely on the audible, forcing the analyst to become an iconoclast. Even in his works on the image, Freud turns to the text, displacing form – again, like Villiers's Edison – through a translation of the image into a verbalized content. There remain, however, fragmentary images – in particular stone ones – dispersed throughout Freud's texts, in particular in *Delusion and Dreams* and *The Moses of Michelangelo*. In a return of the repressed, hypnotic statues appear in studies that oth-

---

[11] In a fast-paced reading of the Freuds' family secrets, Mary Balmary has evoked a chain of associations that point to a Freudian statuomania, and that include Freud's fondness for mushrooms, his regular attendance at performances of *Don Giovanni*, his habit of bringing his figurines to the dinner table, his fascination with Michelangelo's *Moses*, and the choice of Jensen's *Gradiva* as a text that lends itself to a psychoanalytic reading.

erwise promote the primacy of the word, just as the *Venus de Milo* is the underlying image of *L'Eve future*, although she is buried beneath the sediment of masculine verbosity.

Hysterics are, Freud himself readily noted, talking heads, "*Saxa loquuntur!*" (quoted in Gay 192). The hypnotic state of the statue is both a symptom (when self-induced) and a cure (when artificially induced) of hysteria; it petrifies or immobilizes the feminine for analysis. It is, then, a tool for the preservation and exhibition of the repressed history of the individual civilization. The early analyst is both archaeologist and (classical) sculptor: Freud the idealist chisels away the blemishes and warts (symptoms) of the marble block (hysteric) in a move to fabricate a polished facsimile of woman (cured patient). Balmary notes that Freud interprets the hysteric's body as an archaeological site and her symptoms as the "speaking stones" or fragments of an original city, "In the field of ruins that is the body of the hysteric, symptoms are the stones that speak . . . The stone-symptoms speak of a wrong that was done to the city-body" (Balmary 97). Freud the archaeologist has reconstructed or retouched the fragmentary ruins of woman by removing the layers of artifice and exposing a hypnotic ideal.

In his essay on a stone figure that haunted him, Michelangelo's *Moses*, Freud characterizes his method of apprehending art as verbal and interpretive, "But why should the artist's intention not be capable of being communicated and comprehended in *words*, like any other fact of mental life?" (13: 212). Freud then declares that the conversion of images into words is the work of psychoanalysis. Jean-Joseph Goux has characterized this suppression of the image in favor of the word, a "second flight from Egypt," as the inaugural moment of psychoanalysis (138). Moses's passage from ancient Egypt, "land of sphinxes, tombs, and hieroglyphics, land of the imagination and its invasive icons" (138) – land, in short, of statues – to a Judaic interdiction of images is reflected in psychology's passage from the imaginary to the symbolic of psychoanalysis. Freud's retraction of his infamous seduction theory is in part owing to this passage; no longer will the analyst take the hysteric's fantasies (images) at face value. In short, psychoanalysis proclaims the dominance of a paternal desire – representation being maternal (material) – that can only be represented as an effect of language. The Moses statue, itself a representation of the interdiction of images, becomes then a paradoxical flaunting of the attraction of the image. Freud's fascination with this particular statue is due, Goux argues, to the awe of the son before his patricidal act (Michelangelo subverts Moses's law by becoming a sculptor). Thus Freud's essay on the *Moses* reveals a return of the repressed maternal in statuary form and a return of the image to the verbal construction of the Law.

Delusions and Dreams in Jensen's 'Gradiva,' published seven years before *The Moses of Michelangelo*, also turns on a sculptural motif. Whereas the *Moses* essay constitutes a direct analysis of a (masculine) statue, *Delusions and Dreams* ponders a fictional work whose dynamo is a bas-relief representing a female figure. Although Freud does not pay particular attention to *Gradiva*'s sculpted woman, it may be argued that this image haunts him and is resurrected years later, dressed as a man, in the guise of Moses. Indeed, *Delusions and Dreams*, which all but eclipses the ancient bas-relief, is a pre-text to the work on an exemplary piece of Renaissance tomb statuary. Whereas the "primitive" essay reveals an embedded (buried) stone female, the deferred text constructs a discourse on the representation of the male (the symbolic, the father, the Law). *Delusions and Dreams* is, in effect, the *pre-oedipal moment* of the eminently oedipal *Moses of Michelangelo*.[12] The hypnotic bond, of great significance in *Gradiva*, is replaced in *Moses* with the verbal bond of the symbolic, the effect of the successful completion of the oedipal moment.

Freud's first lengthy venture into literary criticism is also the symbolic fulfillment of a wish to revisit Pompeii, a city he had toured in 1902. It is also an example of nineteenth-century-style literary "retrospectivity." Pompeii is a preferred site of Freud's archaeological metaphor, for not only does it represent the slow unearthing required of the digger, but its original layout has been admirably safeguarded by the nature of the trauma it has endured (a volcanic eruption):

> Here [in psychoanalysis] we are regularly met by a situation which with the archaeological object occurs only in such rare

---

[12] In *Gone Primitive*, Marianna Torgovnick exposes Freud's fetish for the sculptural in order to contrast the primitive and civilized in psychoanalysis. Curiously, Torgovnick refers to the *Gradiva* as the *Gravida* throughout her chapter on Freud, allowing her to interpret the bas-relief as a symbol of pregnancy.

> circumstances as those of Pompeii or of the tomb of Tut'ankhamun. All of the essentials are preserved; even things that seem completely forgotten are present somehow and somewhere, and have merely been buried and made inaccessible to the subject. (23: 260)

Again, in *Delusions and Dreams* Freud privileges Pompeii as locus of the unconscious, where the "disappearance of the past [is] combined with its preservation" (9: 51). Pompeii is a representative site of both the repressed and the feminine. In *Gradiva*, the city functions as the analyst's consulting room and as the lost and rediscovered city of woman. A map of Pompeii would correspond both to a diagram of the human psyche and an anatomical chart of the female body, for it is in Pompeii that Jensen's protagonist recovers his sanity and (re)discovers sexual difference.

When the tale opens, Norbert Hanold, Jensen's archaeologist protagonist, is obsessed with the Roman bas-relief of a beautiful woman. Having procured a copy of the work, he speculates upon the history of the young woman and determines to his great distress that she has perished in the Pompeiian catastrophe of 79 A. D. Unaware that his attraction to Gradiva – his name for the image – derives from her resemblance to a childhood friend, Zoe Bertgang, the deluded Hanold travels to Pompeii unconsciously hoping to rescue his ideal from the buried city. Zoe is, fortunately, also visiting Pompeii. She encounters Hanold and is troubled by his strange behavior, for he believes he has found his Gradiva. Zoe, whom Freud will call an analyst, is a keen observer of human nature and realizes the significance of Hanold's bizarre utterances. She successfully cures him during several "hypnotic" scenes by taking Gradiva's place in his mind and thus deflecting his delusion. When Hanold recognizes Zoe he recognizes woman for the first time and his passage from the stone fragment to the living woman is complete.

Freud's reading of *Gradiva* is an analytic *mise en abîme*; the fictional text is analyzed as a case history. The essay is, first and foremost, the transposition of *The Interpretation of Dreams* to a literary text, and Freud begins with a summary of the work on dreams. His reading of *Gradiva* revolves around Hanold's three dreams, which condense and displace Gradiva and Zoe, ancient Pompeii and modern Germany, Latin, Greek, and German. Yet although Freud labels Zoe an analyst, he curiously fails to note that her cure does not require access to these dreams. Zoe's approach is, literally, dynamic or performative; she solves Hanold's riddle by walking before him. As she takes Gradiva's steps, Hanold begins to recognize her as woman. Zoe's cure of Hanold is as much a *walking cure* as it is a *talking cure*. As such, it is a vestige of Freud's hypnotic cure, which may promote the walking trance of the somnambulist.

The sculpted image of the female walk, not the dream passages, becomes the basis for a psychoanalytic cure.[13] As Freud himself points out, the success of Hanold's analysis depends on his translation of the stone figure into the living woman, a translation that recalls Ewald's failed attempt to transfer his love for the *Venus de Milo* onto Alicia Clary. In fact, Ewald must bypass the real woman, Alicia, in order to maintain his hypnotic trance, whereas Hanold is able to successfully superimpose Zoe and the stone woman. In *Gradiva*, the transference requires passage from the Latin *Gradiva* to the German *Bertgang*, "He [the analyst] then brings about something like what Norbert Hanold grasped at the end of the story when he translated back the name 'Gradiva' into 'Bertgang.' The disorder vanishes while being traced back to its origin; analysis, too, brings simultaneous cure" (9: 89). Again, the psychoanalytic method involves the decoding of an image: *Gradiva* and *Bertgang* both mean "the girl who steps along" (9: 11) or "the girl splendid in walking" (Jensen 5). As noted above, Hanold becomes cognizant of this literal translation when he sees Zoe walk. Whereas Freud resembles the tourist who refers to a *written* representation of Pompeii/woman, such as the *Baedecker* guide that Hanold mocks, Hanold privileges the *image* of the city/woman in the form of Zoe's sketchbook. Zoe thus cures Hanold using both the early tools of psychoanalysis (she guides him visually out of his hypnotic trance) and, to some extent, the later ones (she induces him to translate certain key words).

At several points in *Gradiva*, Hanold is described as suffering from a certain lack. Comparing himself to a caged canary, he "was

---

[13] Hanold's second dream does involve a Venus statue. In a Roman hotel, Hanold is irritated by the exaggerated sweetness of his honeymooning neighbors when he falls asleep. Transported to Pompeii on the day of the eruption, he observes an animated *Apollo Belvedere* rescue the *Capitoline Venus* by carrying her off on a rattling cart – an integration into the dream of the honeymooners' squeaking bed. This curious dream recalls the Pygmalion and Commander myths and establishes a connection in Hanold's unconscious between sexuality, death, and sculpture.

thereupon moved by a feeling that he, too, lacked, a nameless something" (Jensen 21). This lack, which lends itself to interpretation in terms of a fetishistic longing,[14] is filled by the superimposed female gaits and then supplemented by an extra detail, one that Freud does not privilege, Zoe's dimple. Hanold sees this facial crease only after he is cured, "[Norbert] noticed for the first time a quite insignificant deviation in the living picture from the stone one. *The latter lacked something* possessed by the former, which appeared at the moment quite clear, a little dimple in her cheek, which produced a slight, indefinable effect" (120, emphasis added). The "insignificant deviation," a wrinkle or fold that defies the polished stone ideal, completes Gradiva/Zoe's passage from stasis to movement. This movement produces the "indefinable effect" of the blemish. The dimple also animates Hanold – it lures him into a kiss. Lack has been successfully projected from Hanold onto the stone woman, allowing Jensen's protagonist to enter into a sexual relationship and persuading Zoe now "more than ever of the complete recovery of [Hanold's] reason" (121).

A valorization of the insignificant detail in the three processes at stake in *Gradiva*, the analytic cure, the literary denouement, and the animation of the image, is quite evident. In *The Moses of Michelangelo*, one discovers a similar authority of the insignificant as that which constitutes the threshold between the static and the dynamic. Freud puts forth an original and controversial thesis in this essay: the historic moment depicted in the statue, he asserts, is not Moses's imminent rise to wrath – as traditional critics have claimed – but rather his self-control, his wrath overcome. In support of this argument, Freud foregrounds two previously ignored details of the *Moses*; first, however, he explains his method through a discussion of accepted notions of the original and reproduction in the art market. A certain Ivan Lermolieff (in reality Giovanni Morelli) has discovered a new and infallible means of recognizing the counterfeit artwork:

---

[14] This is the subject of Bellemin-Noël's *'Gradiva.' Au Pied de la lettre*. The author undertakes a rereading of *Delusions and Dreams* in light of Freud, that is, in terms of the essay on fetishism and subsequent structuralist revisions of Freud. Freud does mention fetishism in *Delusions and Dreams*, but it is not given much weight.

He achieved this by insisting that attention should be diverted from the general impression and main features of a picture, and by laying stress on the significance of minor details, of things like the drawing of the fingernails, of the lobe of an ear, of halos and such undiscovered trifles which the copyist neglects to imitate and yet which every artist executed in his own characteristic way. (13: 222)

This method, a return of the repressed detail, is similar to the psychoanalytic mode of operation, "It, too, is accustomed to divine secret and concealed things from despised or unnoticed features, from the rubbish-heap, as it were, of our observations" (13: 222). Analysis reveals the trifles or details overlooked by the casual observer and it is no accident that these trifles are often physical features and body parts. Physiognomic features such as the dimple are the neglected but crucial signifiers or signatures of the author.[15]

The two details that Freud recovers from the "rubbish-heap" of literature on the *Moses* are "the attitude of his right hand" and "the position of the two Tables of the Law." A close reading of the hand and Tables leads Freud to conclude that the Golden Calf Theory, which interprets the image as ready to awaken, should be replaced by a theory of immobility:

> What we see before us is not the inception of a violent action but the remains of a movement that has already taken place. In his first transport of fury, Moses desired to act, to spring up and take vengeance and forget the Tables; but he has overcome the temptation, and he will now remain seated and still, in his frozen wrath and in his pain mingled with contempt. (13: 229)

Freud's analysis of the statue freezes the castrating father, bearer of the Law. In this version of the oedipal scene, Freud presents the fa-

---

[15] In an essay which uncovers a Freudian theory of the detail in *Screen Memories*, Schor insightfully distinguishes between the use of *detail* and *fragment* in Freud's work. The fragment, apprehended archaeologically, is ancient and constructed and is connoted as masculine. The feminine detail is modern, deciphered, and a product of the verbal (talking cure) and written (literature, case histories) (*Reading* 65-78). I have not made such a distinction in my reading of Freud since I am concerned, precisely, with the details of sculptural fragments. In a footnote to her essay on Duane Hanson, Schor notes that Freud's displacement of sculpture in *The 'Uncanny'* is an "inexplicable move on the part of the author of *The Moses of Michelangelo*" (167n7). Freud performs a similar displacement in *Delusions and Dreams*, from the bas-relief to the dream texts.

ther figure as benign; a violent move would, in fact, cause the Tables to shatter. The essay is, then, a fetishistic attempt to both deny castration (Moses sublimates his aggression toward his "sons") and uphold the Law (the Tables remain intact) at the same moment.

In order to decipher the statue as a frozen moment, Freud must ignore a detail that is for him perhaps *too* significant. This is the stance of Moses's left leg and foot, "raised so that only the toes touch the ground" (13: 214). This position had prompted the "calm before the storm" theory of most critics. But as the statue's insignificant details are highlighted by Freud, the position of the foot, an organ of motion, is reinterpreted as "the *remains* of a movement that has taken place" (emphasis added). Emphasis is shifted vertically along Moses's body from the left foot to the right hand, an appendage valorized by Freud. The fetishistic substitution of one body part for another, the metonymic slide from foot to hand, is clearly represented in the series of drawings that Freud presents as proof of his thesis: the three drawn figures sever Moses at the knee. A fourth figure emphasizes the hand in an exaggerated fashion. Moses is again severed at the knees, he is decapitated, and he loses the left side of his torso. Only his hand, the trifle that upholds the Law, remains intact.

The figures presented by Freud are successive images or frames whose theme is the impulse to movement and its suppression. *Gradiva*'s bas-relief is also implicated in a threesome. Although both Hanold and Freud see only one woman, the Vatican Museum piece represents three female forms in motion, their movements suggesting a certain commonality of purpose. Strikingly, the remains of these images again progressively sever the limbs of the body. Now if one arranges the images of Freud's essay as successive close-ups (1. full view of the *Moses* [frontispiece of the essay]; 2. Freud's second drawing [Moses in motion but without his foot]; and 3. Freud's fourth drawing [a blow-up of the hand]), one finds that the *Gradiva* and *Moses* images may be superimposed. A complete Moses, a Moses who has lost his raised foot, and an exaggerated view of his hand correspond to the three bas-relief figures who are subject to nearly the same process of fragmentation: Gradiva is whole, the second woman lacks her feet (as well as her head) and the third retains only a hand.

This syntagmatic layering of the female and male stone images may be compared to a similar paradigmatic strategy in the written texts. Freud valorizes the detail of the hand by supplanting the meaningful foot and Jensen graduates his protagonist's gaze from the female foot to her hand. The first stage in Hanold's recognition of Gradiva as Zoe occurs when he touches – slaps, actually – the woman's hand to ward off a fly. Towards the end of the tale, he will advance to the face as he takes Zoe's dimple for the same fly and substitutes a kiss for the slap. Along the same vertical lines, Freud shifts emphasis from Moses's foot to his hand and then to his facial expression. His eyes read this progression in reverse, however:

> As our eyes travel *down* it the figure exhibits three distinct emotional strata. The lines of the face reflect the feelings which have won the ascendancy; the middle of the figure shows the traces of suppressed movement; and the foot still retains the attitude of the projected action. *It is as though the controlling influence had proceeded downwards from above.* (13: 230, emphasis added)

Whereas Jensen expresses an upward motion, the rise of desire, Freud's suppression of movement is a call to reason. Hanold succeeds in awakening from his delirium; Moses stays firmly implanted on this throne of controlled desire.

The common detail of the *Gradiva* and *Moses* is the mobile limb, the raised foot, that may in part explain Freud's attraction to Jensen's tale and Michelangelo's work of art. But unlike Freud, who dismisses the foot by divorcing it from Moses's body, Hanold grasps (albeit unconsciously) the crucial significance of this appendage, the signifier that accounts for sexual difference and thus for heterosexuality. Baffled by the foot's peculiar erect position, Hanold first inquires of science:

> The nearly vertical position of the right foot seemed exaggerated; in all experiments which he himself made, the movement left his rising foot always in a much less upright position; mathematically formulated, his stood, during the brief moment of lingering, at an angle of only forty-five degrees from the ground, and this seemed to him natural for the mechanics of walking, because it served the purpose best. Once he used the presence of a young anatomist friend as an opportunity for raising the question, but the latter was not able to deliver a definite decision, as he had made no observations in this connection. He confirmed the experience of his friend, as agreeing with his own, but could not

say whether a woman's manner of walking was different from that of a man, and the question remained unanswered. (9)

The science of anatomy has failed to completely comprehend the female body. Although anatomy would construct woman, certain models (such as Zoe/Gradiva, Hadaly) retain an enigmatic excess. As the text proceeds, Hanold discovers that only Gradiva/Zoe walks in such a peculiar manner. Completely unaware of sexual difference prior to his delusion, Hanold learns from this exceptional detail the same truth that Freud's science will eventually reveal to him: the asymmetry of sexual development. Hanold is now free to pursue his childhood friend not as an all-too-familiar sister, but as a distinct(ly) gendered being.

Delusions and Dreams precedes and foreshadows *The Moses of Michelangelo*. The latter, a masculine text concerning a phallic image, is an inversion or asymmetrical rendering of its pre-text, the feminine bas-relief. Whereas the bas-relief's fetishistic detail implies movement and is the impulse for Gradiva's animation as Zoe, Moses's foot, as observed by Freud, signals an interdiction of movement and a denial of the uncanny quality of sculpture. Freud must at all cost turn away from the foot in order to freeze the statue.[16] In the final analysis, however, another inversion is effected: the masculine *Moses* remains passive, while the feminine *Gradiva* acts out her sexual aggression, permitting Hanold to do so (the name Gradiva recalls the phallic Mars Gradivus, a god of war). Freud's valorization of the Moses statue effects an unexpected return to the maternal in two ways: first, the symbolic yields to the imaginary as a statue becomes the focal point of analysis; second, the statue chosen by Freud represents itself a return of the maternal (as Goux notes, Moses's anger was provoked by the sight of an orgy glorifying incest with the mother [138]). Freud's suppression of this anger leads the

---

[16] In a biographical account of Freud's relation to the Jewish faith that complements Goux's theoretical interpretation, Marthe Robert reads this fear that the inanimate will come to life as an indication of the guilt Freud felt before the father of Judaism, "And despite his fear of punishment, or perhaps because of it, he wished to suffer the rigors of the Law immediately, to have done with his anguished waiting. But he was disappointed: nothing happened, Moses did not move . . . Freud learned once again that he was doomed to bear all the weight of his guilt alone" (144). On *Gradiva* and *Delusions and Dreams*, see also Kofman, *Quatre Romans analytiques*, and Jacobus.

way to a pre-oedipal reunion with the maternal as interdiction in this statue.

Judith Butler's theory of gender as performative illuminates the status (the gender) of these Freudian foots. Butler has shown that gender is an act, literally: it is constituted as a series of performances, it is a "stylized repetition of acts" (140) that reveal its derivative nature. Gender is not natural and performances such as drag demonstrate the purely performative status of gender identity. Certainly, Edison is aware of this truth as he inscribes Hadaly's utterances as a limited series of feminine utterances, or utterances meant to remind Ewald that he is a man. I want to argue now that Gradiva and Moses's steps (and missteps) are performative constructions of gender. In fact, these different acts align quite nicely with Butler's identification of the two taboos that gender "identity" veils: an original taboo against homosexuality and a subsequent incest taboo set up to veil the former prohibition. Moses's interdiction of movement, his desire to cease the performance, is a sign of the interdiction of the mother that veils an original taboo, that of homosexuality, represented by Zoe's aggressive injunction to Hanold that he recognize (and love) her as a woman in the flesh. Sculpture allows Freud to narrate these performances that restrict and restrain sexuality and the production of gender.

Freud's early use of hypnosis was soon replaced by an analytical approach that privileged the symbolic language of the case history. His late essays on the feminine differ greatly in methodology and style from Charcot's *Leçons*. Whereas the French doctor acts out his profession, encouraging and even demanding that the hysteric physically dramatize or perform her illness, the psychoanalyst draws a narrative out of his patients. The passage from the arm (Charcot, Edison) to the foot (Freud) and from the hypnotic image to the decoded confession is crucial. Yet the image does retain a significant importance in Freudian theory. Sculpture, in particular, represents the remnants of the icon that Moses's Tables seek to outlaw. In staging the pre-oedipal and oedipal dramas that Freud translates into words, these two stones do speak, and what they say is revealing.

Saxa loquuntur! – this is Charcot and Freud's intuition and Ewald's dream. The statue's words are symptoms of hysteria to be polished and silenced (made to disappear) by the analyst. Ewald's cure of Alicia rejects the talking cure in favor of the silent statue, for all of the divine bourgeois's talking would never result in a cure.

Ewald is also the subject of a cure in *L'Eve future*, but this cure does not, as in *Gradiva*, require the replacement of the stone woman with a real one; instead, Edison proposes the construction of yet another statue, a gendered being who will not misstep. Edison does not attempt to cure Ewald of his love for the *Venus de Milo,* nor is Alicia capable of providing this remedy. It is Hadaly, finally, who actually cures Ewald. As she describes her mission in the garden scene ("at the cry of your despair, I agreed to dress myself hastily in the radiant forms of your desire, in order to appear before you" [198, 990]), the Lord learns of his origins and is no longer, for the moment, a victim of suicidal delusions. Hadaly the anti-analyst silently reflects him, hypnotically leading him to an understanding of his true self as a seeker of images.

CONCLUSION

As I noted at the beginning of this study, Mary Shelley's early nineteenthy-century monster clearly states his desire for a mate who will have the same defects as himself – she must also be of the monster species. Thus a new Eden will be established with a new order of male and female, "My companion will be of the same nature as myself, and will be content with the same fare. We shall make our bed of dried leaves; the sun will shine on us as on man, and will ripen our food" (157). Edison's successful completion of a future Eve is indeed a sequel to Shelley's text, but what is at stake in *L'Eve future* is of an entirely different order, or gender. Whereas Victor Frankenstein's first and lasting impulse is to reproduce a man, Edison is convinced that the modern world requires an artificial woman – the android is an *andréide* even before Ewald's arrival. These scientists' motives for assembling creatures of the future are vastly different; while the philosopher of science builds the male in order to further his knowledge of "the causes of life" (46), Edison explicitly sets out to *replace* the female sex with his manufactured Eves. Although gender is certainly a significant factor in Frankenstein's decision to construct the male and destroy the female, Edison's endeavor constitutes a general condemnation of women – the completion of the *andréide* entails the annihilation of many flesh and blood human females. The modern couple theorized and fabricated by Edison consists of an artificial female and a human male.

Technologies that converge in the construction of the artificial female body are those that effect a destruction of real women – the image nullifies or invalidates the model. This is especially true of images which technology endows with life, allowing them to circulate and proliferate, that is, *reproduce*: the photosculpted bibelot, the *carte de visite*, and successive photographic frames. These reproductions lose, as Benjamin and Berger point out, authenticity, authority, and aura, as they are deprived of the traditional cult value of the non-reproducible original. But a more emphatic loss is that suffered by the model herself, for modern images do not merely *represent*, they literally *cancel out*. They substitute for women, whose only remaining value is an ability to pose, mimic, and act out. Hadaly is thus a product of modernity's paradoxical enterprise: the preservation of aura in an artificial world.

Hadaly is of a radically different species than Lord Ewald, yet one of her functions is to reflect his nature, in the same way that Frankenstein's Eve would imitate her mate. Although the android is supplemented by the somnambulist, she remains to a certain extent a product of male desire; she is what Ewald would have her be. A mirror of man, she represents the images of desire that he constructs, a synthesis of the *Venus de Milo* and the (maternal) photograph. Ewald's ideal mate is, in effect, a medical patient, a woman who will respond or con-*form* to his every demand as he activates the jewels of her rings and necklace in order to pose her as successive images. Hadaly's escape from these commands is that of death ("*voglio morire*"), but even death is representational as she is killed into art. The "dead" android leaves behind multiple rejuvenated images of the feminine, those which come together in the museum/text that is *L'Eve future*.

L'Eve future's discourse on the interaction between technology and the feminine remains emphatically ambivalent. As powers of metamorphosis and reproduction are appropriated by Edison, and thus by the mechanical, they are both idealized and condemned. The technologically restored *Venus* offers silent beauty, but also death with its skeletal remains. The photograph confers ancestry and history on the individual, at the same time recalling the inevitable aging process, whose ultimate image is death. Proliferation remains closely allied with sterility in *L'Eve future*: "je ne fabriquerai plus d'andréides" is papa Edison's resolve. One birth alone has sufficed to reveal the monstrosity of all women – artificial and real.[1]

---

[1] Kittler reads *L'Eve future* as a pivotal text in the passage from romanticism's need for the One Woman (the mother) to modernity's plurality of women, "only women in plurality remain after Edison's experiment, as discarded experimental material, to be sure, but nonetheless real" (348). One must wonder, then, why Edison foregoes his factory of Eves. In my reading, *L'Eve future*'s status as a threshold text allows it to do both: forego the Woman *and* the women.

CONCLUSION 139

This reading of *L'Eve future* has revealed the ambivalent status of the modern, artificial woman. Born of technologies that strive to restrict the female body to programmed responses before the hypnotist and photographer, among other male masters, she (sometimes) escapes confinement through her dynamic or performative quality. Her enigmatic step, peculiar to anatomists, is the excess that the industrial machine and the machinations of psychoanalysis have been unable to (re)produce and repress. Cros's Virginie, Villiers's Hadaly/Sowana, Charcot's Augustine, and Jensen's Gradiva/Zoe, each abandons the poet and the scientist, enquiring of femininity from experience.

EPILOGUE

When Ewald descends to Hadaly's sepulchral home for the first time, he observes her leaning against a black piano, an artificial bird of paradise perched on her shoulder. Referring to another mechanical bird, a singing nightingale, Hadaly engages Ewald in conversation:

> – It is a lovely voice, is it not, my lord Celian? said Hadaly.
> – Yes, replied Lord Ewald, eyeing curiously the dark, indiscernible figure of the Android. Yes, it is the work of God.
> – Then, she said, you must admire it; but don't try to understand how it is produced.
> – What would be the danger if I tried? Lord Ewald asked, with a smile.
> – God would withdraw from the song! Hadaly murmured placidly. (94-95, 873)

A century later, in a cinematic *mise-en-scène* of the artificial called *Blade Runner*, this scene is repeated. When Deckard first meets the replicant Rachael, she is crossing the room as an owl watches. Rachael asks, "Do you like our owl?" to which Deckard counters, "It's artificial?" "Of course it is," the artificial woman replies. The dialogue has been simplified, the species of bird changed, but the scene is uncannily familiar as the modern couple – male human and female android – meet.

Atop his piano, which Rachael will play, echoing Hadaly's player piano, Deckard has collected old photographs, images of the replicants' – and perhaps his own – ancestors. Photographs endow the androids with the childhood, the history, that they cannot experience during their four year life-span. This artificial heritage, constructed from the images of strangers, is reinforced by implanted memories – "someone else's" past – inscribed (photosculpted?) onto the replicants. Photography is one example of the vast array of visual mechanisms which define knowledge, truth, and origin in *Blade Runner*. The technical art that contributed to the definition of the nineteenth-century's future Eve is taken to its limit in the film, as it becomes *the* signifier of humanity, registering origin and history, ancestry and the aging process, life and death, thus providing artificial answers to Deckard's Gauguinesque questions, "Where do I come from? Where am I going? How long have I got?"

Rachael points to her maternal lineage as evidence of her humanity. She shows Deckard a photo of a young girl, herself, she argues, with her mother. But it is, again, the male who is most obsessed with the construction of maternal ancestry. Deckard returns to this photo several times during the film, as Barthes continually turns to his image of the feminine. It would appear, in fact, that the sight of the photograph intensifies Deckard's love for Rachael, who becomes desirable *because* he possesses her image, however fabricated. Furthermore, he accepts Rachael as he comes to *recognize* her as the child, as he comes to believe that she too is of woman born. It is noteworthy that Deckard's own origin is unclear; like Ewald, he has no family to our knowledge except an ex-wife (an Alicia?). As he ponders Rachael's photo he seems to long to enter the picture, to become the third figure who will oedipalize and thus humanize both himself and Rachael.

Blade Runner abounds in references to the family, the maternal, and fertility. Although the film would appear to relegate reproduction entirely to genetic technologies and mechanics, traditional images of the family write themselves into the story. In one telling scene, Deckard uses a complex video machine to enlarge a portion of a photograph belonging to the replicant Leon. This photo is different from the others; in it, Leon's hotel room, not his ancestry, is depicted. As Deckard enlarges the photo he glimpses first the fragment of a male android, a fist, then a female replicant reclining on a sofa. The latter image must be blown up from a bit of the mirror which hangs over a dresser. Zhora is not present within the frame of the apparatus, but reflected from behind the photographer. This photo is a play on a well-known Renaissance painting that is saturated with symbols of marriage and fertility: Jan Van Eyck's *Arnolfini Wedding* (1434). In the painting, a bride – stomach protruding – and groom stand in a bedchamber facing the witness/painter who is reflected along with an assistant in an oval mirror on the back wall. Leon's photo is a modern version, a revision of this canvas. Maternity is banished, however, from this scene – no one (not even replicants) stands in the room, all the viewer sees are bits and pieces of technology's prowess, an artificial arm and an obscured female android, as Deckard further fragments the image with his machine.

Furthermore, maternity and technological repoduction are associated in Rachael's fabricated memories. Deckard recites two of these: first, a young girl plays doctor with her brother – a typical upbringing with its moment of recognition of sexual difference is thus established. Second, the girl watches a spider egg hatch, which prompts one hundred babies to emerge and engulf the mother. This last memory is an indictment of the mother as harbinger of (here, her own) death. In fact, the very first scene of the film associates maternity, representation, and death. When Leon is asked to talk about his mother by the (Freudian) examiner, he says, "My mother? Let me tell you about my mother." He then draws a gun and shoots his interviewer. Mothers give birth to engulfing creatures and provoke violent actions in *Blade Runner*; although they are necessary providers of an individual past, they remain monstrous representations.

Although *Blade Runner* narrates the stories of several replicants of both genders, it is, not surprisingly, a female who defies her maker. As Deckard says, "Rachael was special. No termination date." Unlike the other replicants, Rachael maintains a more human – that is less certain – relationship to time and death, perhaps because the maternal image she possesses is so close to animation. At the end of the film, she and Deckard fly north over mountains, leaving the Los Angeles of 2019 AD, their fate unknown. Eerily, but not unexpectedly, they imitate Edison's photogenic and statuesque "machine à fabriquer l'idéal" and her human lover, who set out to sea together.[2]

---

[2] The ultimate denouements of the two stories differ, of course. On *L'Eve future* and *Blade Runner*, see Doane "Technophilia."

WORKS CITED

Agulhon, Maurice. *Marianne into Battle.* Trans. Janet Lloyd. Cambridge: Cambridge UP, 1981.
———. "La 'Statuomanie' et l'histoire." *Ethnologie française* 7-8 (1977-78): 145-72.
Anzalone, John. "*Danse macabre*: le pas de deux Villiers-Baudelaire." *Jeering Dreamers: Villiers de L'Isle-Adam's* L'Eve future *at our Fin de Siècle.* Ed. John Anzalone. Amsterdam: Rodopi, forthcoming.
———. "Golden Cylinders: Inscription and Intertext in *L'Eve future.*" *L'Esprit créateur* 26.4 (1986): 38-47.
———. Ed. *Jeering Dreamers:* L'Eve future *autour de la fin de siècle.* Amsterdam: Rodopi, forthcoming.
Armes, Roy. "Entendre, c'est comprendre: In Defence of Sound Reproduction." *Screen* 29.2 (1988): 8-22.
Auerbach, Nina. *Woman and the Demon. The Life of a Victorian Myth.* Cambridge, MA: Harvard UP, 1982.
Bal, Mieke. *Reading* Rembrandt. *Beyond the Word-Image Opposition.* Cambridge: Cambridge UP, 1991.
Balmary, Marie. *Psychoanalyzing Psychoanalysis. Freud and the Hidden Fault of the Father.* Trans. Ned Lukacher. Baltimore: Johns Hopkins UP, 1982.
Balzac, Honoré de. *The Unknown Masterpiece.* Trans. Michael Neff. Berkeley: Creative Arts Book Company, 1984.
———. *Sarrasine.* Barthes, *S/Z.* Paris: Seuil, 1970.
Barrucand, Dominique. *Histoire de l'hypnose en France.* Paris: PUF, 1967.
Barthes, Roland. "Le Message photographique." *L'Obvie et l'obtus.* Paris: Seuil, 1982.
———. *Camera Lucida. Reflections on Photography.* Trans. Richard Howard. New York: Hill and Wang, 1981.
———. *S/Z.* Trans. Richard Miller. New York: Hill and Wang, 1974.
Baudelaire, Charles. *Correspondance.* Ed. Claude Pichois. Vol. 2. Paris: Gallimard, 1973. 2 vols.
———. *The Letters of Charles Baudelaire to his Mother. 1833-1866.* Trans. Arthur Symons. New York: Benjamin Blom, 1971.
———. *Art in Paris. 1845-1862. Salons and Other Exhibitions.* Trans. Jonathan Mayne. Oxford: Phaidon, 1965.
———. *The Painter of Modern Life and Other Essays.* Trans. Jonathan Mayne. London: Phaidon, 1964.
———. *The Poems in Prose.* Vol. 2. Trans. Francis Scarfe. London: Anvil Press Poetry, 1989. 2 vols.

Beale, Arthur. "A Technical View of Nineteenth-Century Sculpture." *Metamorphosis in Nineteenth-Century Sculpture.* Ed. Jeanne L. Wasserman. Cambridge, MA: Harvard UP, 1975.
Beizer, Janet. *Ventriloquized Bodies. Narratives of Hysteria in Nineteenth-Century France.* Ithaca: Cornell UP, 1994.
Bellemin-Noël, Jean. Gradiva. *Au Pied de la lettre.* Paris: PUF, 1983.
———. "Notes sur le fantastique (Textes de Théophile Gautier)." *Littérature* 8 (1972): 3-23.
Bellour, Raymond. "Ideal Hadaly." *Camera Obscura* 15 (1986): 110-35.
Benjamin, Walter. "The Work of Art in the Age of Mechanical Reproduction." *Illuminations.* Ed. Hannah Arendt. Trans. Harry Zohn. New York: Harcourt, Brace and World, 1968.
Berger, John. *Ways of Seeing.* London: BBC, 1972.
Bernheimer, Charles. *Figures of Ill Repute. Representing Prostitution in Nineteenth-Century France.* Cambridge, MA: Harvard UP, 1989.
Blade Runner. Dir. Ridley Scott. The Ladd Company, 1982.
Bloy, Léon. "La Résurrection de Villiers de l'Isle-Adam." *L'Oeuvre complète de Léon Bloy.* Paris: François Bernouard, 1947.
Boime, Albert. *Hollow Icons. Politics of Sculpture in Nineteenth-Century France.* Kent, OH: Kent State UP, 1987.
Borch-Jacobsen, Mikkel. *The Freudian Subject.* Trans. Catherine Porter. Stanford: Stanford UP, 1988.
Borowitz, Helen O. *The Impact of Art on French Literature. From Scudéry to Proust.* Newark: U of Delaware P, 1985.
Bourneville, D.-M and Paul Régnard. *Iconographie photographique de la Salpêtrière.* 1875. Text not distributed. Bibliothèque Charcot, Salpêtrière.
———. *Iconographie photographique de la Salpêtrière.* Paris: Delahaye & Lecrosnier. 1876-1880. 3 vols.
Bowie, T. R. *The Painter in French Fiction.* Chapel Hill: U of North Carolina P, 1950.
Bungay, Stephen. *Beauty and Truth. A Study of Hegel's Aesthetics.* Oxford: Oxford UP, 1984.
Burnham, Jack. *Beyond Modern Sculpture. The Effects of Science and Technology on the Sculpture of this Century.* New York: Braziller, 1968.
Butler, Judith. *Gender Trouble. Feminism and the Subversion of Identity.* New York: Routledge, 1990.
Carrouges, Michel. *Les Machines célibataires.* Paris: Chêne, 1976.
Chambers, Ross. "L'Ange et l'automate; variations sur le mythe de l'actrice de Nerval à Proust." *Archives des lettres modernes* 128 (1971): 3-80.
———. "Gautier et le complexe de Pygmalion." *Revue d'histoire littéraire de la France* 72 (1972): 641-58.
Charcot, J.-M. *L'Hystérie.* Ed. E. Trillat. Toulouse: Privat, 1971.
———. *Oeuvres complètes.* Ed. D.-M Bourneville, et al. Vols. 1-9. Paris: Lecrosnier & Babé, 1886-93. 9 vols.
———. *Leçons du mardi à la Salpêtrière. Policlinique.* Ed. Blin, Charcot, and Colin. Paris: Delahaye & Lecrosnier, 1887-88.
———. *Leçons du mardi à la Salpêtrière. Policlinique.* Ed. Blin, Charcot, and Colin. Paris: Lecrosnier & Babé, 1888-89.
Charcot, J.-M and Paul Richer, eds. *Les Démoniaques dans l'art.* Paris: Macula, 1984.
———. *Les Difformes et les malades dans l'art.* Paris: Lecrosnier and Babé, 1889.
Compère, Daniel. "Les Monstres nouveaux." *Romantisme* 41 (1983): 91-99.
Conyngham, Deborah. *Le Silence éloquent. Thèmes et structures de* L'Eve future *de Villiers de l'Isle-Adam.* Paris: Corti, 1975.

Coste, Didier. "Où Jules Verne montre son jeu: *Le Château des Carpathes* comme allégorie de la communication narrative." *Revue des lettres modernes* (1983): 161-78.
Cros, Charles. *Oeuvres complètes*. Ed. Louis Forestier. Paris: Gallimard, 1970.
Daireaux, Max. *Villiers de l'Isle-Adam*. Paris: Desclée de Brouwer, 1936.
Damisch, Hubert. *Fenêtre jaune cadmium ou les dessous de la peinture*. Paris: Seuil, 1984.
Derrida, Jacques. *De la Grammatologie*. Paris: Minuit, 1967.
———. *La Vérité en peinture*. Paris: Flammarion, 1976.
Didi-Huberman, Georges. *L'Invention de l'hystérie. Charcot et l'iconographie photographique de la Salpêtrière*. Paris: Macula, 1982.
Doane, Mary Ann. "Technophilia: Technology, Representation and the Feminine." *Body Politics: Women and the Discourses of Science*. Ed. Mary Jacobus, et al. New York: Routledge, 1990.
———. "The Voice in the Cinema: The Articulations of Body and Space." *Yale French Studies* 60 (1980): 33-50.
Filoche, Jean-Luc. "*Le Chef-d'oeuvre inconnu*: peinture et connaissance." *L'Année Balzacienne* ns 1 (1980): 47-59.
Flaubert, Gustave. *Dictionary of Accepted Ideas*. Trans. Jacques Barzun. New York: New Directions, 1954.
Fosca, François. *De Diderot à Valéry: Les Ecrivains et les arts visuels*. Paris: Albin Michel, 1960.
Foucault, Michel. *The Birth of the Clinic. An Archaeology of Medical Perception*. Trans. A. M. Sheridan Smith. New York: Pantheon Books, 1973.
———. *The History of Sexuality*. Vol. 1. Trans. Robert Hurley. New York: Pantheon Books, 1978.
Freud, Sigmund. *The Standard Edition of the Complete Psychological Works*. Ed. and Trans. James Strachey, et al. London: Hogarth, 1953-74. 24 vols.
Galassi, Peter. *Before Photography: Painting and the Invention of Photography*. New York: Museum of Modern Art, 1981.
Gasché, Rodolphe. "The Stelliferous Fold: On Villiers de l'Isle-Adam's *L'Eve future*." *Studies in Romanticism* 22 (1983): 293-327.
Gautier, Théophile. *Mademoiselle de Maupin*. New York: Modern Library, 1950.
———. *La Photosculpture*. Paris: Dupont, 1864.
———. *Récits fantastiques*. Paris: Flammarion, 1981.
———. *Le Roman de la momie*. Paris: Flammarion, 1966.
Gay, Peter. *Freud. A Life For Our Time*. New York: W. W. Norton, 1988.
Gilbert, Sandra and Susan Gubar. *The Madwoman in the Attic. The Woman Writer and the Nineteenth-Century Literary Imagination*. New Haven: Yale UP, 1979.
Godfrey, Sima. "Mummy Dearest: Cryptic Codes in Gautier's *Pied de momie*." *Romanic Review* 75.3 (1984): 302-11.
Goux, Jean-Joseph. *Symbolic Economies. After Marx and Freud*. Trans. Jennifer Curtiss Gage. Ithaca: Cornell UP, 1990.
Grasso, Luciana. "La 'Fantaisie pompéienne' de Gautier: *Arria Marcella*." *Bulletin de la Société Théophile Gautier* 6 (1984): 93-108.
Haraway, Donna. "A Manifesto for Cyborgs: Science, Technology, and Socialist Feminism in the 1980s." *Coming to Terms. Feminism, Theory, Politics*. Ed. Elizabeth Weed. New York: Routledge, 1989.
Heath, Stephen. *The Sexual Fix*. New York: Schocken Books, 1984.
Hedges, Inez. "The Myth of the Perfect Woman: Cinema as Machine Célibataire." *L'Esprit Créateur* 26.4 (1986): 26-37.
Hegel, Georg Wilhelm Friedrich. *Aesthetics: Lectures on Fine Art*. Vol. 2. Trans. T. M. Knox. Oxford: Clarendon, 1975. 2 vols.

Huet, Marie-Hélène. *Monstrous Imagination*. Cambridge, MA: Harvard UP, 1993.
Huysmans, J.-K. *A Rebours*. Paris: Gallimard, 1977.
Huyssen, Andreas. "Mapping the Postmodern." *Feminism/Postmodernism*. Ed. Linda J. Nicholson. New York: Routledge, 1990.
———. "The Vamp and the Machine: Technology and Sexuality in Fritz Lang's *Metropolis*." *New German Critique* 24-25 (1981-82): 221-37.
Irigaray, Luce. *This Sex Which is Not One*. Trans. Catherine Porter with Carolyn Burke. Ithaca: Cornell UP, 1985.
———. *Speculum of the Other Woman*. Trans. Gillian C. Gill. Ithaca: Cornell UP, 1985.
Jacobus, Mary. *Reading Woman. Essays in Feminist Criticism*. New York: Columbia UP, 1986.
Jensen, Wilhelm. *Gradiva*. Trans. Helen M. Downey. New York: New Republic, 1927.
Johnson, Barbara. "My Monster/Myself." *A World of Difference*. Baltimore: Johns Hopkins UP, 1987.
Kittler, Friedrich A. *Discourse Networks. 1800/1900*. Trans. Michael Metteer with Chris Cullens. Stanford: Stanford UP, 1990.
Kofman, Sarah. *Quatre Romans analytiques*. Paris: Galilée, 1973.
Konrad, Linn B. "Villiers de l'Isle-Adam's Future Eve: A Textual Phoenix." *Romance Quarterly* 34.2 (1987): 147-54.
———. "The Woman's Role in Villiers de l'Isle-Adam's Search for the Ideal." *Nineteenth-Century French Studies* 13.2-3 (1985): 113-25.
Lacan, Jacques. *The Four Fundamental Concepts of Psychoanalysis*. Ed. Jacques-Alain Miller. Trans. Alan Sheridan. New York: Norton, 1978.
———. *Encore*. Paris: Seuil, 1975.
———. *Ecrits I*. Paris: Seuil, 1966.
Lathers, Marie. "The Decadent Goddess: *L'Eve future* and the *Venus de Milo*." *Jeering Dreamers: Villiers's* L'Eve future *at Our Fin de Siècle*. Ed. John Anzalone. Amsterdam: Rodopi, forthcoming.
———. "*L'Eve future* and the Hypnotic Feminine." *The Romanic Review*. 84.1 (1993): 43-54.
———. "Modesty and the Artist's Model in *Le Chef-d'oeuvre inconnu*." *Symposium: A Quarterly Journal in Modern Foreign Literatures* 46.1 (1992): 49-71.
———. "Snapshots of a Future Eden." *Australian Journal of French Studies* 28.1 (1991): 50-59.
———. "Picturing the Ideal Feminine: Photography in Nineteenth-Century Literature." *Yearbook of Interdisciplinary Studies in the Fine Arts* 2 (1991): 357-66.
Lauretis, Teresa de. *Technologies of Gender. Essays on Theory, Film, and Fiction*. Bloomington: Indiana UP, 1987.
Lebensztejn, Jean-Claude. *ZigZag*. Paris: Flammarion, 1981.
Lebois, André. *Villiers de l'Isle-Adam révélateur du verbe*. Neuchâtel: H. Messeiller, 1952.
Lemagny, Jean-Claude and André Rouillé, eds. *A History of Photography. Social and Cultural Perspectives*. Trans. Janet Lloyd. Cambridge: Cambridge UP, 1987.
Lessing, Gotthold. *Laocoön*. Trans. William A. Steel. London: J. M. Dent and Sons, 1930.
Londe, Albert. *La Photographie médicale*. Paris: Gauthier-Villars et fils, 1893.
Matlock, Jann. *Scenes of Seduction. Prostitution, Hysteria and Reading Difference in Nineteenth-Century France*. New York: Columbia UP, 1994.
McCauley, Elizabeth Anne. *A. A. E. Disdéri and the Carte de Visite Portrait Photograph*. New Haven: Yale UP, 1985.
Mérimée, Prosper. "The Venus of Ille." *Prosper Mérimée*. Trans. George Burnham Ives. New York: G. P. Putnam's Sons, 1903.

Michelson, Annette. "On the Eve of the Future: The Reasonable Facsimile and the Philosophical Toy." *October* 29 (1984): 3-21.
Miller-Frank, Felicia. *The Mechanical Song: Women, Voice and the Artificial in Nineteenth-Century French Narrative.* Stanford: Stanford UP, 1995.
Milner, Max. *La Fantasmagorie. Essai sur l'optique fantastique.* Paris: PUF, 1982.
Moers, Ellen. "Female Gothic." *Literary Women.* New York: Oxford UP, 1985.
Mulvey, Laura. "Visual Pleasure and Narrative Cinema." *Visual and Other Pleasures.* London: The Macmillan Press LTD, 1989.
Mustière, Philippe. "La Chambre au miroir ou l'appropriation de l'être dans *Le Château des Carpathes.*" *Littérature* 43 (1981): 43-50.
Neefs, Jacques. "*Le Château des Carpathes* et la question de la représentation." *Jules Verne et les sciences humaines.* Paris: Union Générale d'Editions, 1979.
Noiray, Jacques. *Villiers de l'Isle-Adam. Jules Verne.* Vol. 2 of *Le Romancier et la machine: L'Image de la machine dans le roman français (1850-1900).* Paris: Corti, 1981-3. 2 vols.
Ortner, Sherry B. "Is Female to Male as Nature Is to Culture?" *Woman, Culture, and Society.* Ed. Michelle Zimbalist Rosaldo and Louise Lamphere. Stanford: Stanford UP, 1974.
Petchesky, Rosalind Pollack. "Foetal Images: the Power of Visual Culture in the Politics of Reproduction." *Reproductive Technologies. Gender, Motherhood and Medicine.* Ed. Michelle Stanworth. Minneapolis: U of Minneapolis P, 1987.
"La Photosculpture." *Grand dictionnaire Larousse.* Paris, 1874.
Praz, Mario. *Mnemosyne: The Parallel Between Literature and the Visual Arts.* Princeton: Princeton UP, 1970.
Quatremère de Quincy, Antoine C. "A Commentary on an Antique Statue of Venus Found on the Island of Milos." *From the Classicists to the Impressionists.* Ed. Elizabeth Holt. New York: New York UP, 1966.
Raitt, A. W. *The Life of Villiers de l'Isle-Adam.* Oxford: Clarendon, 1981.
Read, Herbert. *The Art of Sculpture.* London: Faber and Faber, 1954.
Rifelj, Carol de Dobay. "*La Machine humaine*: Villiers' *L'Eve future* and the Problem of Personal Identity." *Nineteenth-Century French Studies* 20. 3-4 (1992): 430-51.
———. "Minds, Computers and Hadaly." *Jeering Dreamers: Villiers de L'Isle-Adam's L'Eve future at our Fin de Siècle.* Ed. John Anzalone. Amsterdam: Rodopi, forthcoming.
Robert, Marthe. *From Oedipus to Moses: Freud's Jewish Identity.* Trans. Ralph Manheim. Garden City, NY: Anchor Books, 1976.
Rollet, Pascal. "Expression et répression d'une voix féminine résistante dans *L'Eve future* de Villiers de l'Isle-Adam." *Jeering Dreamers: Villiers de l'Isle-Adam's L'Eve future at our Fin de Siècle.* Ed. John Anzalone. Amsterdam: Rodopi, forthcoming.
Rose, Marilyn Gaddis. "Two Misogynist Novels: A Feminist Reading of Villiers and Verne." *Nineteenth-Century French Studies* 9 (1980-81): 117-23.
Rosen, Charles and Henri Zerner. *Romanticism and Realism. The Mythology of Nineteenth-Century Art.* London: W.W. Norton, 1984.
Roustang, François. *Psychoanalysis Never Lets Go.* Trans. Ned Lukacher. Baltimore: The Johns Hopkins UP, 1983.
Saisselin, Rémy. *The Bourgeois and the Bibelot.* New Brunswick, NJ: Rutgers UP, 1984.
Schefer, Jean-Louis. "Du Simulacre à la parole." *Tel Quel* 31 (1967): 85-91.
Schor, Naomi. *Reading in Detail. Aesthetics and the Feminine.* New York: Methuen, 1987.
———. "Dreaming Dissymmetry: Barthes, Foucault, and Sexual Difference." *Men in Feminism.* Ed. Alice Jardine and Paul Smith. New York: Methuen, 1987.

Schor, Naomi. *Breaking the Chain. Women, Theory and French Realist Fiction.* New York: Columbia UP, 1985.
Schuerewegen, Franc. "*Fin-de-siècle Télétechnè*: Villiers de l'Isle-Adam and Jules Verne." *Modernity and Revolution in Late Nineteenth-Century France.* Ed. Barbara T. Cooper and Mary Donaldson-Evans. Newark: U Delaware P, 1992.
Serres, Michel. "Un Dieu de stade: M. Alphonse." *Alphonse Juillard: d'une passion l'autre.* Ed. Brigitte Cazelles and René Girard. Saratoga, CA: ANMA Libri, 1987.
———. *Statues.* Paris: François Bourin, 1987.
———. *Genèse.* Paris: Grasset, 1982.
———. *Feux et signaux de brume: Zola.* Paris: Grasset, 1975.
———. *Jouvences sur Jules Verne.* Paris: Minuit, 1974.
Shelley, Mary. *Frankenstein, or the Modern Prometheus.* New York: Modern Library, 1984.
Silverman, Kaja. *The Acoustic Mirror. The Female Voice in Psychoanalysis and Cinema.* Bloomington: Indiana UP, 1988.
Solomon-Godeau, Abigail. *Photography at the Dock. Essays on Photographic History, Institutions, and Practices.* Minneapolis: U Minnesota P, 1991.
———. "The Legs of the Countess." *October* 39 (1986): 65-107.
Sontag, Susan. *On Photography.* New York: Farrar, Straus and Giroux, 1977.
Steiner, Wendy. *The Colors of Rhetoric. Problems in the Relation Between Modern Literature and Painting.* Chicago: U of Chicago P, 1982.
Steinmetz, Jean-Luc. "Gautier, Jensen et Freud." *Europe* 601 (1979): 50-57.
Tatar, Maria M. *Spellbound: Studies on Mesmerism and Literature.* Princeton: Princeton UP, 1978.
Torgovnick, Marianna. *Gone Primitive. Savage Intellects, Modern Lives.* Chicago: U of Chicago P, 1990.
Verne, Jules. *Carpathian Castle.* Ed. I. O. Evans. Westport, CT: Associated Booksellers, 1963.
Villiers de l'Isle-Adam. *Tomorrow's Eve.* Trans. Robert Martin Adams. Urbana: U of Illinois P, 1982.
———. *Eve of the Future Eden.* Trans. Marilyn Gaddis Rose. Lawrence, KS: Coronado Press, 1981.
———. *Oeuvres complètes.* Vol. 1. Ed. Pierre-Georges Castex and Alan Raitt. Paris: Gallimard (Pléiade), 1986. 2 vols.
———. *Sardonic Tales.* Trans. Hamish Miles. New York: Alfred A. Knopf, 1927.
Wallen, Jeffrey. "The End of Illusion in *L'Eve future.*" *Modernity and Revolution in Late Nineteenth-Century France.* Ed. Barbara T. Cooper and Mary Donaldson-Evans. Newark: U Delaware P, 1992.
Warner, Marina. *Monuments and Maidens. The Allegory of the Female Form.* New York: Atheneum, 1985.
Websters Third New International Dictionary. s.v. aesthetics, artifice, artificial, aura, bibelot.
Williams, Rosalind H. *Dream Worlds. Mass Consumption in Late Nineteenth-Century France.* Berkeley: U of California P, 1982.
Zola, Emile. *Nana.* Paris: Garnier-Flammarion, 1968.

NORTH CAROLINA STUDIES IN THE ROMANCE LANGUAGES AND LITERATURES

I.S.B.N. Prefix 0-8078-

Recent Titles

RABELAIS: HOMO LOGOS, by Alice Fiola Berry. 1979. (No. 208). -9208-4.

"DUEÑAS" AND DONCELLAS": A STUDY OF THE DOÑA RODRÍGUEZ EPISODE IN "DON QUIJOTE", by Conchita Herdman Marianella. 1979. (No. 209). -9209-2.

PIERRE BOAISTUAU'S "HISTOIRES TRAGIQUES": A STUDY OF NARRATIVE FORM AND TRAGIC VISION, by Richard A. Carr. 1979. (No. 210). -9210-6.

REALITY AND EXPRESSION IN THE POETRY OF CARLOS PELLICER, by George Melnykovich. 1979. (No. 211). -9211-4.

MEDIEVAL MAN, HIS UNDERSTANDING OF HIMSELF, HIS SOCIETY, AND THE WORLD, by Urban T. Holmes, Jr. 1980. (No. 212). -9212-2.

MÉMOIRES SUR LA LIBRAIRIE ET SUR LA LIBERTÉ DE LA PRESSE, introduction and notes by Graham E. Rodmell. 1979. (No. 213). -9213-0.

THE FICTIONS OF THE SELF. THE EARLY WORKS OF MAURICE BARRES, by Gordon Shenton. 1979. (No. 214). -9214-9.

CECCO ANGIOLIERI. A STUDY, by Gifford P. Orwen. 1979. (No. 215). -9215-7.

THE INSTRUCTIONS OF SAINT LOUIS: A CRITICAL TEXT, by David O'Connell. 1979. (No. 216). -9216-5.

ARTFUL ELOQUENCE, JEAN LEMAIRE DE BELGES AND THE RHETORICAL TRADITION, by Michael F. O. Jenkins. 1980. (No. 217). -9217-3.

A CONCORDANCE TO MARIVAUX'S COMEDIES IN PROSE, edited by Donald C. Spinelli. 1979. (No. 218). 4 volumes, -9218-1 (set), -9219-X (v. 1), -9220-3 (v. 2); -9221-1 (v. 3); -9222-X (v. 4).

ABYSMAL GAMES IN THE NOVELS OF SAMUEL BECKETT, by Angela B. Moorjani. 1982. (No. 219). -9223-8.

GERMAIN NOUVEAU DIT HUMILIS: ÉTUDE BIOGRAPHIQUE, par Alexandre L. Amprimoz. 1983. (No. 220). -9224-6.

THE "VIE DE SAINT ALEXIS" IN THE TWELFTH AND THIRTEENTH CENTURIES: AN EDITION AND COMMENTARY, by Alison Goddard Elliot. 1983. (No. 221). -9225-4.

THE BROKEN ANGEL: MYTH AND METHOD IN VALÉRY, by Ursula Franklin. 1984. (No. 222). -9226-2.

READING VOLTAIRE'S CONTES: A SEMIOTICS OF PHILOSOPHICAL NARRATION, by Carol Sherrnan. 1985. (No. 223). -9227-0.

THE STATUS OF THE READING SUBJECT IN THE "LIBRO DE BUEN AMOR", by Marina Scordilis Brownlee. 1985. (No. 224). -9228-9.

MARTORELL'S TIRANT LO BLANCH: A PROGRAM FOR MILITARY AND SOCIAL REFORM IN FIFTEENTH-CENTURY CHRISTENDOM, by Edward T. Aylward. 1985. (No. 225). -9229- 7.

NOVEL LIVES: THE FICTIONAL AUTOBIOGRAPHIES OF GUILLERMO CABRERA INFANTE AND MARIO VARGAS LLOSA, by Rosemary Geisdorfer Feal. 1986. (No. 226). -9230-0.

SOCIAL REALISM IN THE ARGENTINE NARRATIVE, by David William Foster. 1986. (No. 227). -9231-9.

HALF-TOLD TALES: DILEMMAS OF MEANING IN THREE FRENCH NOVELS, by Philip Stewart. 1987. (No. 228). -9232-7.

POLITIQUES DE L'ECRITURE BATAILLE/DERRIDA: le sens du sacré dans la pensée française du surréalisme à nos jours, par Jean-Michel Heimonet. 1987. (No. 229). -9233-5.

GOD, THE QUEST, THE HERO: THEMATIC STRUCTURES IN BECKETT'S FICTION, by Laura Barge. 1988. (No. 230). -9235-1.

THE NAME GAME. WRITING/FADING WRITER IN "DE DONDE SON LOS CANTANTES", by Oscar Montero. 1988. (No. 231). -9236-X.

When ordering please cite the *ISBN Prefix* plus the last four digits for each title.

Send orders to: University of North Carolina Press
P.O. Box 2288
CB# 6215
Chapel Hill, NC 27515-2288
U.S.A.

NORTH CAROLINA STUDIES IN THE ROMANCE LANGUAGES AND LITERATURES

I.S.B.N. Prefix 0-8078-

Recent Titles

GIL VICENTE AND THE DEVELOPMENT OF THE COMEDIA, by René Pedro Garay. 1988. (No. 232). -9234-3.
HACIA UNA POÉTICA DEL RELATO DIDÁCTICO: OCHO ESTUDIOS SOBRE "EL CONDE LUCANOR", por Aníbal A. Biglieri. 1989. (No. 233). -9237-8.
A POETICS OF ART CRITICISM: THE CASE OF BAUDELAIRE, by Timothy Raser. 1989. (No. 234). -9238-6.
UMA CONCORDÃNCIA DO ROMANCE "GRANDE SERTÃO: VEREDAS" DE JOÃO GUIMARÃES ROSA, by Myriam Ramsey and Paul Dixon. 1989. (No. 235). Microfiche, -9239-4.
CYCLOPEAN SONG: MELANCHOLY AND AESTHETICISM IN GÓNGORA S "FÁBULA DE POLIFEMO Y GALATEA", by Kathleen Hunt Dolan. 1990. (No. 236). -9240-8.
THE "SYNTHESIS" NOVEL IN LATIN AMERICA. A STUDY ON JOÃO GUIMARÃES ROSA'S "GRANDE SERTÃO: VEREDAS", by Eduardo de Faria Coutinho. 1991. (No. 237). -9241-6.
IMPERMANENT STRUCTURES. SEMIOTIC READINGS OF NELSON RODRIGUES' "VESTIDO DE NOIVA", "ÁLBUM DE FAMÍLIA", AND "ANJO NEGRO", by Fred M. Clark. 1991. (No. 238). -9242-4.
"EL ÁNGEL DEL HOGAR". GALDÓS AND THE IDEOLOGY OF DOMESTICITY IN SPAIN, by Bridget A. Aldaraca. 1991. (No. 239). -9243-2.
IN THE PRESENCE OF MYSTERY: MODERNIST FICTION AND THE OCCULT, by Howard M. Fraser. 1992. (No. 240). -9244-0.
THE NOBLE MERCHANT: PROBLEMS OF GENRE AND LINEAGE IN "HERVIS DE MES", by Catherine M. Jones. 1993. (No. 241). -9245-9.
JORGE LUIS BORGES AND HIS PREDECESSORS OR NOTES TOWARDS A MATERIALIST HISTORY OF LINGUISTIC IDEALISM, by Malcolm K. Read. 1993. (No. 242). -9246-7.
DISCOVERING THE COMIC IN "DON QUIXOTE", by Laura J. Gorfkle. 1993. (No. 243). -9247-5.
THE ARCHITECTURE OF IMAGERY IN ALBERTO MORAVIA'S FICTION, by Janice M. Kozma. 1993. (No. 244). -9248-3.
THE "LIBRO DE ALEXANDRE". MEDIEVAL EPIC AND SILVER LATIN, by Charles F. Fraker. 1993. (No. 245). -9249-1.
THE ROMANTIC IMAGINATION IN THE WORKS OF GUSTAVO ADOLFO BÉCQUER, by B. Brant Bynum. 1993. (No. 246). -9250-5.
MYSTIFICATION ET CRÉATIVITÉ DANS L'OEUVRE ROMANESQUE DE MARGUERITE YOURCENAR, par Beatrice Ness. 1994. (No. 247). -9251-3.
TEXT AS TOPOS IN RELIGIOUS LITERATURE OF THE SPANISH GOLDEN AGE, by M. Louise Salstad. 1995. (No. 248). -9252-1.
CALISTO'S DREAM AND THE CELESTINESQUE TRADITION: A REREADING OF CELESTINA, by Ricardo Castells. 1995. (No. 249). -9253-X.
THE ALLEGORICAL IMPULSE IN THE WORKS OF JULIEN GRACQ: HISTORY AS RHETORICAL ENACTMENT IN LE RIVAGE DES SYRTES AND UN BALCON EN FORÊT, by Carol J. Murphy. 1995. (No. 250). -9254-8.
VOID AND VOICE: QUESTIONING NARRATIVE CONVENTIONS IN ANDRÉ GIDE'S MAJOR FIRSTPERSON NARRATIVES, by Charles O'Keefe. 1996. (No. 251). -9255-6.
EL CÍRCULO Y LA FLECHA: PRINCIPIO Y FIN, TRIUNFO Y FRACASO DEL PERSILES, por Julio Baena. 1996. (No. 252). -9256-4.
EL TIEMPO Y LOS MÁRGENES. EUROPA COMO UTOPÍA Y COMO AMENAZA EN LA LITERATURA ESPAÑOLA, por Jesús Torrecilla. 1996. (No. 253). -9257-2.
THE AESTHETICS OF ARTIFICE: VILLIERS'S L'EVE FUTURE, by Marie Lathers. 1996. (No. 254). -9254-8.

When ordering please cite the ISBN Prefix plus the last four digits for each title.

Send orders to: University of North Carolina Press
P.O. Box 2288
CB# 6215
Chapel Hill, NC 27515-2288
U.S.A.